FIXING
FAIRNESS

FIXING FAIRNESS

4 Tenets to Transform
Diversity Backlash
into Progress for All

LILY ZHENG

Berrett-Koehler
PUBLISHERS

Berrett-Koehler Publishers, Inc.
1333 Broadway, Suite P100
Oakland, CA 94612-1921
(510) 817-2277
bkconnection.com

ORDERING INFORMATION
Quantity sales. Special discounts are available on quantity purchases by corporations, associations, and others. For details, please go to bkconnection.com to see our bulk discounts or contact bookorders@bkpub.com for more information.
Individual sales. Berrett-Koehler publications are available through most bookstores. They can also be ordered directly from Berrett-Koehler: (800) 929-2929; bkconnection.com.
Orders for college textbook / course adoption use. Please contact Berrett-Koehler: (800) 929-2929.

Distributed to the US trade and internationally by Penguin Random House Publisher Services.

The authorized representative in the EU for product safety and compliance is EU Compliance Partner, Pärnu mnt. 139b-14, 11317 Tallinn, Estonia, www.eucompliancepartner.com, +372 5368 65 02.

Berrett-Koehler and the BK logo are registered trademarks of Berrett-Koehler Publishers, Inc.

Printed in the United States of America

Berrett-Koehler books are printed on long-lasting acid-free paper. When it is available, we choose paper that has been manufactured by environmentally responsible processes. These may include using trees grown in sustainable forests, incorporating recycled paper, minimizing chlorine in bleaching, or recycling the energy produced at the paper mill.

Cataloging-in-Publication Data is on file at the Library of Congress.
Library of Congress Control Number: 2025027311
ISBN 9798890571410 (hardcover) | ISBN 9798890571427 (pdf) | ISBN 9798890571434 (epub)

First Edition
33 32 31 30 29 28 27 26 25   10 9 8 7 6 5 4 3 2 1

Book production: Happenstance Type-O-Rama
Cover design: Ashley Ingram
Author photo: Richard DeVaul

To advocates, activists, leaders, and changemakers everywhere still looking for permission to do and be more than the status quo. Go get 'em.

CONTENTS

Introduction   1

1 Catching Cobras   15

2 Transforming the Backlash   35

3 Fairness Is Environmental   53

4 Access Is Good Design sans Duct Tape   73

5 Inclusion Is Solidarity at Scale   91

6 Representation Is Leadership You Trust   109

7 The Future of Fairness   127

   Notes   137
   Acknowledgments   147
   Index   149
   About the Author   161

INTRODUCTION

In the United States and in several other countries around the world, diversity, equity, and inclusion are in the crosshairs. As I write this, the United States government continues to engage in flagrant disregard for the rule of law, dismantling and undermining the public sector, defunding institutions of higher learning, eroding civil rights protections, and intimidating the private sector. Along the way, right-wing extremists looking for a convenient boogeyman to justify their attacks jumped on the acronym of "DEI," recasting the previously mundane acronym into a caricature of anti-American values.

In the United States, conversations about DEI in 2026 feel dramatically more high stakes than they did in 2016. Social media discussions of DEI regularly devolve into shouting matches and finger-pointing. Employers, many of which sponsored DEI-related work for decades, increasingly run every activity with any likelihood of being perceived as "DEI" by their general counsel and communications team for fear of backlash.

It's easy to get the feeling that the defining spirit of these times has shifted from hope to cruelty. That the foundational belief of a pluralistic democratic society—the recognition that *everyone deserves dignity, respect, and opportunity* regardless of the beliefs, values, needs, circumstances, experiences, and perspectives we hold—is no longer commonly held by the majority. That the window of acceptable behavior has shifted so far that exclusion, discrimination, and open malice have become "a tolerable point of view."

If you were to estimate what proportion of Americans agree with a pro-diversity statement like "racial diversity benefits the country," what would you guess? Close your eyes for a moment and make an estimate.

In a study run by researchers at the University of Wisconsin–Madison that asked the same question in response to fifteen pro-diversity statements, they found that guesses from American participants drawn from all walks of life and all political affiliations clustered around 55 percent.[1] Was your personal estimate lower, higher, or around the same?

Now here's the twist. *The vast majority of them underestimated support for DEI.* The actual average amount of support for pro-DEI statements? A whopping 82 percent. The overwhelming majority of respondents simultaneously supported diversity while worrying that they might hold a minority belief.

I could not make up a more hopeful fact than this one. In fact, it's so hopeful that the current state of our polarized nation makes me almost intolerably outraged. To allow the minority of those committed to hate and exclusion to sow division, reverse progress, limit our potential, and create a future that 82 percent of us object to as a fait accompli—as if we have no say over it—is absolutely unacceptable.

There's a good chance that if you're reading this book, you're a member of that 82 percent. You might not agree with every initiative under the DEI umbrella, or believe that all work calling itself DEI has been executed well. You might have questioned, written off, or ignored DEI as irrelevant or performative. *But you certainly don't believe in the discriminatory, unequal, and cruel vision that right-wing extremists put forth as sacrosanct.*

In my work with dozens of workplace and community leaders over the last five years, this exact sentiment has been our starting point. And as anxious as leaders often are to express it, the belief in the value of a fair, nondiscriminatory, and respectful workplace, community, and world is shared by more people than they think. Where the work gets hard, though, is what happens after that starting point.

The reality is that this book would not need to exist if the solution to anti-DEI backlash, fear, and polarization was to simply tell people that diversity, equity, and inclusion are more popular than they think. For one thing, this fact wouldn't even be quite correct because being pro-diversity isn't the same thing as being pro-DEI.

A Pew Research Center survey in 2024 found that support for workplace DEI—referring to the acronym, and not just "diversity" in the abstract—had dropped to just above 50 percent among Americans.[2] A Post-Ipsos study that same year found that while 69 percent of their respondents supported the work of DEI when given a definition of diversity, equity, and inclusion, support fell to 61 percent when respondents evaluated just the acronym on its own.[3]

What these studies tell us is that even though support for the goals of diversity, equity, and inclusion may be widespread, *the way workplaces pursue DEI* is very much still contentious. So contentious, in fact, that it's become a liability easily exploited by bad-faith actors looking to undermine American institutions in the name of "fighting DEI."

Many advocates make the point that popularity shouldn't be the primary factor behind whether organizations support or do DEI. I agree—it's effectiveness that matters most. As I advise leaders, it's less important that an initiative is popular if it doesn't succeed at what it was designed to achieve. It's less important that an initiative is unpopular if it regularly succeeds at achieving its goals.

So what of workplace DEI, then? Popularity aside, does it actually benefit people?

A YouGov poll conducted in early 2025 looked into exactly this question, asking respondents what effect workplace diversity, equity, and inclusion programs had had on them, whether positive, negative, or neutral. Without knowing the results, if you were to guess what percentage of people fall into each category, what would you say?

Personally, I guessed around 50 percent of people would feel like workplace DEI had a positive effect on them, that 20 percent felt that it had a negative effect, and that 30 percent or so would feel ambivalent.

I was extremely wrong.

The results were stunning: while only 16 percent shared that DEI had harmed them, a similarly meager 20 percent indicated that DEI had positively impacted them, with the largest group—more than 60 percent combined—responding with "no effect" or "don't know" (see figure 1).[4] Across all ages, genders, regions, and political orientations surveyed, this overall pattern held true. Even among the group with the highest perception of benefit, Black respondents, just 34 percent felt that they had benefited from workplace DEI; 59 percent felt no effect or weren't sure.

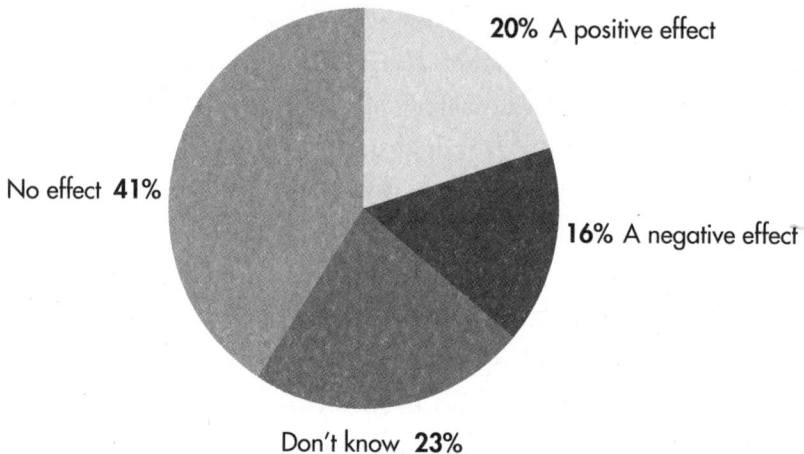

20% A positive effect

16% A negative effect

Don't know 23%

No effect 41%

Adapted from a YouGov survey of 6,419 US adults conducted on January 23, 2025

FIGURE 1. What Effect Have Diversity, Equity, and Inclusion (DEI) Programs Had on You Personally?

To the vast majority of people, workplace DEI was neither harmful nor beneficial. It was just simply ineffective, and by virtue of that ineffectiveness, irrelevant.

This is the painful truth about workplace DEI that goes under-recognized, even as in the United States and in other countries around the world the debate around the "ideology" of DEI continues. The ideological debate ought to be a nonstarter. Practically everyone believes that workplaces free from discrimination, where people feel safe and respected, and that are rich in perspectives and experiences are better than the alternative. Remember, 82 percent of people believe in the value of diversity, even if they underestimate others' support. Anti-DEI arguments get their peculiar staying power not from the workplace DEI's *unpopularity*, but from its perceived ineffectiveness and irrelevance.

Workplace DEI leaders and practitioners have lost control of the narrative.

When they think about "DEI," workers *ought* to think about their workplace's progress toward achieving greater diversity, equity, and inclusion. They ought to think about their improved parental leave benefits, physically accessible offices, and respectful working environment. They ought to think about the workplace well-being policies that protect their health and dignity, the fair decision-making processes that give them a voice in the decisions that get made, and the universal design processes adopted by their product teams that result in products and services accessible to and appreciated by many.

The workers I engage with don't think of those things. Instead, they're more likely to recall the cultural heritage celebrations put on by overworked volunteers that they are too busy to attend, the yearly employee engagement survey that never gets followed up on, the mandatory training they sit through while paying the minimum possible attention, or the motivational speaker wasting sixty minutes of their day without making a dent in the overwork, petty politics, and discrimination they face as part of their standard workday.

"DEI?" they say to me. "You mean when our CEO made that commitment to 'racial equity' on social media, indefinitely postponed the pay equity audit they promised, and then laid off thousands of our junior colleagues, most of whom weren't White? *That* DEI?"

And as the political environment continues to shift against DEI, workers are increasingly likely to recall and repeat radicalizing rhetoric that makes the case that workplace DEI actively *harms* them, along with misinformation about DEI efforts being unmeritocratic, engaging in "reverse discrimination," and so on, even though that information couldn't be further from reality.

"DEI?" they say to me. "You mean our illegal use of racial quotas, discrimination against White people, and suppression of free speech? *That* DEI?"

Whereas mainstream DEI's reputation among the indifferent majority in the mid-2010s may have been "harmless but useless," it's increasingly becoming "useless *and possibly harmful.*" As polarization worsens, leaders have to contend with internal DEI initiatives that struggle to achieve success; competing expectations and misconceptions from disengaged, skeptical, or even hostile employees, customers, and investors; a regulatory environment that becomes more contradictory and risky by the day; and a cultural context where every communication is guaranteed to enrage someone.

Many of my colleagues in the workplace DEI space see this moment as a time for ideological courage. I have heard no shortage of rallying cries exhorting leaders to "hold the line," to "keep the faith," to "believe that diversity will win."

The perspective I share in this book is different. My guiding values have always been rooted in practical progress, not abstract ideology. I don't help leaders "express their commitment to diversity," I help them build stronger, more fair, more effective, and more resilient workplaces that bring in, retain, and draw out the potential of the best talent, wherever it lies. I don't lecture workers to "do the right thing"; I build processes that make collaboration, ethical behavior, and accountability easier and more effective than the alternative. I don't tell people to "believe in the value of inclusion"; I change workplaces to make inclusion the default for everyone by building a culture that rewards respect, upholds safety, and makes everyone feel valued for what they bring to the table.

Bravery alone will not reverse the slow-motion train wreck of workplace collapse that has occurred over the last decade. In the United States today, 66 percent of workers experience burnout,[5] 76 percent of workers indicate at least one symptom of a mental health condition,[6] worker engagement has dropped to a 10-year low of 31 percent,[7] and 91 percent of workers have experienced discrimination of some kind.[8]

It was this bad when DEI was popular, when hashtags were flooding social media and every company had unconscious bias training. It continues to be this bad now that DEI is under attack, DEI language quietly disappears from shareholder reports, and DEI training evaporates. If we care about progress, then we don't have the luxury to treat the presence or absence of visible DEI initiatives as anything more than signposts of their popularity. What we have to do is double down on *making real progress to help real people*, whatever form that takes.

To me, the answer is clear. The practices and beliefs that got us into this crisis cannot be the practices and beliefs that get us out of it, and so the only viable future I see for DEI is one in which it no longer resembles DEI as we know it.

Fixing Fairness is about what comes after DEI: what I call the FAIR Framework, standing for Fairness, Access, Inclusion, and Representation, and made up of four pillars that collectively articulate a vision and strategy beyond the acronym. Each of the components of FAIR stands for an outcome that *everyone* deserves to experience: everyone deserves fairness;

everyone deserves to access products, services, and environments; everyone deserves to feel included; everyone deserves to feel represented.

The four pillars are mandates for how FAIR work gets done, to ensure it differentiates itself from ineffective and performative DEI efforts. All FAIR work must

- Focus on outcomes and results, not good intentions.

- Change the workplace environment, not just the people in it.

- Activate coalitions involving everyone, not cliques of shared ideology.

- Leverage the unity of win-win, not the division of zero-sum.

I came by these pillars through deep research. Over nearly a decade of experience embedded within organizations large and small, poring over scientific research literature, and talking with workers from as wide a range of backgrounds as you could imagine, I came by four fundamental flaws with legacy DEI efforts, and four fundamental solutions that the best and most effective DEI practitioners were already using.

The flaws?

Fixating on inputs and good intentions, so that we uplift passion, commitment, and visibility—and ignore whether the problems that drive us to action ever end up solved through our efforts.

Thinking too narrowly about the project of DEI as one of self-help or self-improvement, so that we overprescribe self-reflection and individualized learning as tools of behavior change—and ignore the powerful incentives and social norms within our environments that keep the status quo where it is.

Mistaking the tactics of safety and comfort for those of changemaking, so that we seek similarity, sameness, and agreement in our own movements—at the cost of building broader coalitions across our differences with the power to actually make a difference.

Gravitating toward zero-sum and antagonistic language, so that we platform rhetoric that makes us feel good ("It's justice for you to get less and for me to get more!")—at the cost of activating the very backlash that will inevitably undermine what progress we make.

These flaws may not be present in every DEI program, and yet just about everyone that has interacted with workplace DEI has experienced them. That's why many DEI leaders and practitioners in my network, even in the mid-2010s, were already advocating for change and pushing for more accountability, more integration of DEI into business operations, more coalition building, and more effectiveness. The emergence of anti-DEI backlash only accelerates this desperately needed evolution.

The FAIR Framework is my answer for "what comes next?" It lays out the north star and standard that leaders and practitioners doing DEI ought to have held themselves up to from the start, and proposes inversions and solutions to the four flaws of legacy DEI.

Instead of passion, commitment, and visibility alone, FAIR guides us to celebrate real, measurable results. Within FAIR work, the unassuming manager able to create an inclusive team environment is venerated over the inspirational speaker equipped only with flowery language on the value of inclusion.

Instead of seeing individual people as the problem, FAIR guides us to change our environment. Within FAIR work, the focus is on building the capacity of any community or organization to change its environment, rather than the capacity of any one individual to change themselves.

Instead of treating social identity—our race, gender, sexuality, class, disability, and so on—as walls that isolate our communities, FAIR guides us to apply and understand our differences for collective benefit. Within FAIR work, ideological purity, identity essentialism, maximalism, perfectionism, and other common pitfalls movements can become trapped by (more on these later in the book) are seen as challenges to solve rather than flaws to tolerate.

And finally, instead of taking pride in the zero-sum, all-or-nothing, and blame-and-shame approaches that have so dogged legacy DEI efforts, FAIR guides us instead to focus unflinchingly on the universal benefit of a better world for everyone in it, with abundance—not scarcity—as the objective. Within FAIR work, everyone has a role to play, everyone benefits, and even though the work might be hard, everyone gets to feel good about making progress.

For those who have consistently led their organizations and communities through this work successfully, the FAIR Framework articulates a vision that is nearly indistinguishable from the highest standard of DEI done right. Over the course of developing the framework, I've been teased by my mentors and fellow practitioners who have said things like "*New* framework? Guess I was ahead of the game!" or "Doesn't *everyone* do DEI like this already?"

But for those who have seen DEI as a simple exercise in public relations, an easy opportunity to make a quick buck or quickly gain prestige or validation, or an uncritical service simply provided to meet the demands of corporate clients, the FAIR Framework will feel like an almost impossible bar to meet. Privately, practitioners and leaders have messaged me with their anxieties about the challenge of evolving their legacy DEI efforts to meet the FAIR standard. "Even if these practices don't work, they're my entire business model. What should I do?" "You're asking for the impossible. *No one* could possibly do DEI the way you talk about it."

And yet, many people already do. The point of the FAIR Framework is to make the highest standard of yesterday's DEI work the new minimum bar to meet, in the face of malicious backlash, workplaces in crisis, and ever-increasing expectations from customers, communities, and investors that will collectively eat a poorly implemented DEI program for breakfast.

Ineffective tactics, rhetoric of "retribution against" rather than "reconciliation with," the safety of inaction over the fear of making mistakes, and prioritizing the comfort of ideological sameness over the messiness of coalition are all glaring liabilities for any workplace leader or practitioner in 2026 and beyond. These leaders will face heavy scrutiny from internal and external constituents alike and be forced to constantly manage backlash and conflict.

But leaders who can defuse polarization, facilitate healthy conflict, build accountability for making things right when harm occurs, unite and rally people across their differences to solve shared problems for the benefit of all, and enforce standards of respect, safety, and value in a world that often fails to do so? *They will win.* Their organizations will weather the culture wars around DEI by keeping people focused on shared purpose and shared benefit. Their people, in experiencing a standard of (working) life that maintains respect, safety, and value across people's different beliefs and identities; prevents discrimination and mistreatment; and equips everyone to succeed, will reward the organization with their thriving.

Throughout this book, I outline the pragmatic strategy we all need to build a world where we can thrive and succeed free from discrimination and mistreatment, and share the tactics we can use to take us there with today's fractured, polarized, angry, and scared world as the starting point.

I'll tell the story of how, for a workforce and a society in which fairness was long lacking, legacy DEI failed to fix what was broken, building instead an entire industry devoted to empty talk and ineffective action. I'll share how shortcuts taken and missteps made by generations of well-meaning workplace leaders and DEI practitioners steadily decoupled the DEI industry from the real progress workers, marginalized groups, and society at large desperately needed, and sowed the seeds for the pendulum swing of backlash to erase the small gains it eked out. Specifically, I'll explain how legacy DEI lost its way when it became defined by good intentions without accountability, individual "self-help" over systems change, intra-identity cliques over inter-identity coalitions, and zero-sum over win-win communications—and the catastrophic consequences of this failure.

I'll lay out what we can do instead to actually solve the problems so many of our organizations and communities face, if not the familiar motions of legacy DEI. I'll introduce and outline the FAIR Framework and its four tenets: outcomes over intentions, environment over individuals, coalitions over cliques, and abundance over scarcity. I'll present a path forward for how leaders, practitioners, and ordinary people can avoid being swept up by the endless DEI "culture wars," and best apply their limited time and energy to creating real change. I'll put each of the letters of the FAIR Framework into practice, from Fairness to Access to Inclusion to Representation, using real-world examples showing how each letter of the acronym can evolve its legacy DEI equivalent into something far more effective.

I'll share how we need to evolve our perception of fairness from "lack of bias in individual behaviors" into fair *environments* that mitigate the potential for bias to cause harm from the start. By focusing on how commonly accepted realities of our modern workplace might actually be *unfair* to the vast majority of workers, I'll show how *fairness* can become the motivating principle behind the evolution of legacy DEI, and explore the surprising potential of work that builds fairer systems, rather than trying to make fairer people.

I'll show how expanding access for all, far from a back-burner DEI issue, should be thought of as one of the smartest investments we can make in our collective thriving. To truly achieve access in workplaces where everyone's needs differ, we'll need to flip our understanding of this work on its head: redistributing our efforts from reactive accommodations for those outside the "average" toward proactive universal and inclusive design in recognition that the "average person" doesn't even exist. I'll share how the powerful ideas of the curb-cut effect and targeted universalism can deliver massive returns that improve the quality of experience for everyone, and how we can put those ideas into practice.

I'll present a new vision for inclusion, the only outcome I've chosen to carry over from the acronym "DEI," that can shift us out of shallow celebrations of minority identity into focused application of *everyone's* identities to organize across our differences. I'll show how recognizing what sets us *apart* can become the foundation for change if we can draw on those differences to come *together* in service to building better workplaces for all. I'll give voice to common critiques of modern-day identity-based movements and put forward a vision and practices for how we might build better coalitions, drive better movements, and achieve more progress for everyone because of it.

I'll challenge you next with a fundamental reframing of representation, redefining it as an outcome inherently tied to *trust* in leadership, rather than demographic box-checking. I'll lay out how the well-meaning focus on demographic representation that has so defined legacy DEI has led to the proliferation of tokenism and box-checking as the default, and make the case for a new approach to building a more representative world beyond the confines of the zero-sum conversation that's defined us for so long.

This book is my best guidance for you, reader, on how we can all make it through the anti-DEI headwinds we may face and solve legacy DEI's biggest shortcomings at the same time. It's my challenge to all of us to rise above the cyclical nature of progression and regression that's defined this work for more than a half century and put our own power and influence to use to make a difference through collective action.

As you read this book, I want you to think of yourself as a change-making leader and practitioner, even if that's not a job title you've ever held. As you read this book, I want you to adopt the mindset of someone who isn't just looking to learn more information, but is looking to *achieve more by doing better*. You may not agree with everything I share here, or find every tool useful for your unique context. That's to be expected. My hope is that by engaging critically and pragmatically with this book and taking from it as much as you can, you might better defend, extend, and accelerate the positive impact you make in the world.

Let's begin.

1

CATCHING COBRAS

In colonial India, or so a famous anecdote goes, the British colonial government was looking for a way to solve a cobra infestation in the city of Delhi. British leaders devised a simple but brilliant plan: they would offer a bounty on dead cobra heads. By incentivizing everyday people to kill cobras, the British hoped to solve the overpopulation problem and address poverty at the same time.

Not long after the bounty was announced, cobra heads were being delivered by the dozen every day and the cobra population started to fall. The scheme was working! But those short-term gains were not to be. After many months the infestation was still present, yet more and more heads were being submitted every day. Why?

It turned out that the source of steady income from the cobra bounty was simply too great an opportunity for anyone to ignore. Faced with the possibility of the cobra problem—and this highly reliable income stream— disappearing, entrepreneurial citizens decided to *start breeding cobras*.

It made enormous sense. Catching and killing wild cobras was far more challenging than breeding them and killing them in captivity. And so cobra farms sprang up en masse as a direct result of the simple incentives the British had devised, and the problem these incentives aimed to solve simply persisted unabated.

But the story doesn't end there. When the British caught wind that citizens were breeding cobras to kill and hand in, they grew enraged at the thought that they were being taken advantage of—"tricked" out of their money. So they made the most obvious short-term decision they could think of: they canceled the cobra bounty.

Immediately, every cobra farm's business model collapsed. With no reason to breed and kill their now-worthless cobras in captivity, the cobra farmers reacted with the only obvious decision they could think of: *they released their captive cobras into the city*. The wild cobra infestation exploded to levels far worse than they had started off.

This is the most famous example of what is now called the "cobra effect": when well-intentioned solutions cause unintended consequences that enable or even worsen the original problem.

There are cobra effects all around us in the 21st century. Policymakers choosing to widen highways to reduce congestion enabled greater urban sprawl and greater demand on highways, which then created even worse congestion. Decision-makers for the NFL implementing a rule awarding a higher draft order for teams with worse performance during the previous season drove teams to purposely lose games. City leaders levying a tax on thin plastic bags to reduce pollution led to retailers switching to using much thicker plastic bags to skirt the tax—dramatically increasing plastic pollution.

It's easy to write these stories off as comedic incompetence. "Well, of course the cobra farms would set their cobras loose," you might be thinking. "Of course coaches would intentionally throw games to get a higher draft order in the following season." With the clarity of hindsight, it's easy to imagine that we ourselves would make different choices in the same scenarios.

But the truth is more uncomfortable. Unintended consequences are the shadow behind every effort to intentionally change complicated systems, and when decision-makers are under pressure to *do something* and act quickly, cobra effects are virtually inevitable, even for the most experienced and thoughtful leaders. Show me a leader who has "never" caused unintended consequences through their decisions and I'll show them some excellent self-awareness exercises to help them introspect more effectively.

I have plenty of my own experiences with cobra effects, including a memorable one from the very start of my career as an inclusion educator in the mid-2010s while working with university staff to communicate respectfully with students from all backgrounds.

The people I worked with were a compassionate bunch. They cared deeply about the students they worked with, but their environment often made respectful communication a time-consuming consideration that was often overlooked.

Staff were failing to communicate respectfully with students because they weren't taking the time to deeply understand students' needs and see each student as their own person. This wasn't entirely their fault—they were often so overworked that taking the time to personalize their interactions with students could compromise their ability to carry out their core job responsibilities. And yet, unless they slowed down, the problem would persist. In workshop after workshop, I stressed the importance of asking thoughtful questions, accepting the possibility of not always getting it right, and building trusting relationships over time. If external constraints and expectations got in the way, they needed to advocate for themselves and set better expectations to prioritize engaging with students well, rather than engaging with students quickly.

My workshop attendees never liked this answer. Over and over again, they pressed me for quick tools they could use without much effort while on the go. They wanted lists of "do's and don'ts" of words and practices that they should or shouldn't use for each social identity group (by race, gender, sexuality, disability, religion, nationality, and so on) and other bite-sized practices that promised big impact without fundamentally changing the status quo.

I pushed back, at least at first. There are very few silver bullets in this work that could achieve what these professionals were looking for because no community is a monolith. Even if two students hold the same social identity, there is no guarantee that they will find the same set of words or practices respectful. For this reason, oversimplified lists of "best practices" run a high risk of unintentionally doing more harm than good. Think of a social group that you belong to: if I asked both you and one other member of that group to give me a list of five "do's and don'ts" for that group, are you confident that your answers would be the same?

And yet all the same, I was under enormous pressure from this group to help them do *something*. Even though I knew it wasn't going to fix the root cause of the problem, after hearing the same requests for weeks on end and feeling insecure about my own work as a young professional, I caved and compiled the lists of "do's and don'ts" I was asked for.

"These are 'better' practices, not 'best' practices," I cautioned when sharing the resources I had put together. "Use discretion and adapt these practices as needed depending on your goals and your audience." I'm not sure how many people actually heard me, but even then, I told myself that change happened one step at a time—that something was better than nothing.

Months later, I heard a complaint from a student. A well-intentioned staff person, in a room full of students, had pointedly interrupted the flow of conversation during an event to ask this student—but no others—to share their gender pronouns. It was a cringeworthy attempt at gender inclusion, but it landed far more painfully than an ignorant comment shared in passing might have. Because the staff person singled out the student in front of their peers, the student felt forced to self-disclose their gender identity with all eyes on them in a setting where they wouldn't necessarily have chosen to do so on their own. The comment made them feel isolated, anxious, and excluded—the exact opposite of what the staff person ostensibly intended.

The student seemed shocked as they shared the complaint with me. "If [the staff person] had just been ignorant like everyone else, it would have been hard enough," they elaborated later to me. "But to almost get it right, but do so in the exact wrong way . . . somehow, that makes it feel worse."

The staff person involved became defensive when I brought up the incident, after receiving the student's permission to pass on their comments. "When you don't know someone's pronouns, you should ask," the staff member repeated. "Wasn't that included in the resource list you had shared?"

I still remember how my stomach lurched.

The poet Alexander Pope famously wrote, "A little learning is a dangerous thing," and in this moment I fully understood his meaning. The staff member had been looking for a quick and easy practice related to gender inclusion that they could use without needing to change their overall behavior. In my belief that "something was better than nothing," I had provided them with exactly that resource, which they had then (mis)used to marginalize and upset a student. The result, regardless of the staff person's good intentions, was harm—and I had played an unwitting part in it!

In choosing to take the path of least resistance to meet the "want" that my workshop attendees expressed, pressured by my own insecurity and desire to be helpful, I had given people an oversimplified resource *and* the overconfidence to use it widely, without the guardrails to do so safely or effectively. Regardless of my own intentions or the circumstances I was operating in, my "solution" failed to solve the problem I set out to address. If anything, I might have just supercharged the potential for everyday people to make problems worse.

When I later started my own practice as an independent DEI consultant, the contours of this story continued to haunt me.

With my very first client, a midsize tech company, leaders paid me to develop a diversity training—before I learned through talking to their employees that the whole project was a diversionary effort to give the impression that leaders were doing *something*, just not the pay-equity audit employees had been demanding for years. When I suggested to my contacts that the audit would likely make a far bigger impact and solve a far bigger problem than a training could, I received an email a week later informing me that we would no longer be working together.

With a finance company, I offered a discount to pair an employee assessment (that would allow us to understand the extent of inequality and exclusion within the organization) with the one-hour workshop they had initially requested. They agreed to the proposal and I delivered the workshop, after which my contact let slip that the whole reason they had worked with me was to spotlight the workshop in their internal newsletter to promote their company's DEI commitment. When I followed up a week later to discuss the employee assessment, I was ghosted. To this day, years later, they still have yet to respond to my last email (or pay me for the second part of our contract).

With a health-care company, a potential assessment project fell through at the last minute after a squabble between myself and one of their executives over the questions in the assessment. "We can't ask the questions you're proposing," he said bluntly in our final meeting. "If we ask them, and we find problems, that sets the expectation that we do something about it." I was so stunned by his comment that I forgot to set my face, and stared wide eyed at him over the video call for several seconds. "Isn't the point of an assessment to do something about what you find?" I ended up blurting out, to which he made a noncommittal grimace that instantly told me everything I needed to know.

There's a pattern to these stories, and it's not just that I should have done better diligence in vetting clients and structuring contracts: it's that organizations' enormous appetite for "DEI activities" rarely, if ever, corresponds with "DEI impact," and practitioners are caught in the middle. Torn between our desire to make an impact that actually helps people and our need to make a living, we often tell ourselves exactly what I did—that *something is better than nothing*—and talk ourselves into willingly helping leaders draft empty words, design ineffective initiatives, and put on flashy but ultimately low-impact events.

The leaders in these stories tell themselves that they're acting rationally. Caught between their own aversion toward large-scale organizational change and the demands articulated by their employees or customers who want clear signals of change on a short timeline, leaders tell themselves that "something is better than nothing." They seek out solutions that are most likely to placate their critics without requiring long-term commitment or lavish budgets. What lies at that intersection are well-crafted (yet empty) words, highly promoted (yet ineffective) initiatives, and flashy (yet low-impact) events.

Everyone gets what they want—unhappy workers get a quick fix, leaders get an easing of pressure, and consultants get paid—and yet no one gets what they need. Discrimination persists. Unfair environments stay unfair. The problems that initiated these efforts are simply kicked down the road until they rear their heads again, at which point the whole process starts again with workers who are a little less trusting, practitioners who are a little more jaded, and leaders who are a little more defensive, and on, and on.

How did we get here?

The Enshittification of Workplace DEI

Facebook, the social media platform, hit 100 million users in 2008. Its runaway popularity came from its vibrant user base, who signed up for the platform to stay connected with their friends, peers, classmates, colleagues, and family members. Facebook was where you learned about a cousin's wedding, kept up with your long-distance friends, griped about schoolwork with your classmates, and stayed in touch with your work buddies.

In 2026, Meta, which owns Facebook, former rival platform Instagram, WhatsApp, and a number of other companies, is valued at more than $1.5 trillion. And yet, scrolling through your feed (if you still even use it), your experience might differ somewhat from how it might have been in 2008. Sponsored posts and ads clutter your feed. Outraging, AI-generated, or nonsensical posts, reels, and other content from people you've never heard of fill the page, served up by an algorithm expertly tuned to keep you on the site. The updates from your friends and family members are buried under an avalanche of this content, to the point where the experience of navigating the platform becomes excruciating enough for you to consider leaving the platform altogether. The thing is, many people already have. Facebook's daily active users have been dropping since 2022.

Canadian journalist and author Cory Doctorow, writing in 2023, made the compelling argument that Facebook's decline in quality was not an accident. Instead, it was the inevitable result of an intentional set of decisions—the same decisions now frequently pursued by many other platforms across the internet ecosystem—made by leaders committed more to short-term value extraction rather than long-term value creation.

"Here is how platforms die: first, they are good to their users; then they abuse their users to make things better for their business customers; finally, they abuse those business customers to claw back all the value for themselves. Then, they die."[1]

Doctorow calls this cycle *enshittification*: the gradual degradation of online platforms as a result of profit seeking via exploitation. It starts when a platform builds a strong user base by creating outsized value, often delivered unsustainably, for the people utilizing it. In the tech playbook, this often means taking a good idea, designing a world-class experience that hooks users to a platform built around it, and accelerating that process by hypersubsidizing the user experience with venture capitalist money and operating at a loss to displace competitors. Think of how cheaply Uber, Lyft, and Airbnb offered their services in the first few years of operation.

The buzz and interest soon draw vendors to the platform—advertisers, sellers, and so on—who seek value from the prime audience of loyal users. At first, platforms eagerly work to create value for these vendors, ensuring that their ads seamlessly reach users and easily hooking the vendors to the platform just as users were hooked previously. Eventually, with the platform now having carved out a powerful niche for itself, both users and vendors become caught: neither can leave, because they've come to rely on the platform for needs that only that platform can meet. With Facebook, for example, users rely on the platform to connect with their friends and family members, while advertisers rely on the ad revenue from those users. With Amazon, users rely on the marketplace to buy everything they need, and sellers rely on users who have come to buy things only from Amazon and nowhere else.

Then, with entirely captive audiences of both users and vendors without comparable alternatives, the platforms show their true colors. With no more incentive to focus on quality or deliver additional value, platforms shift their focus to squeezing more and more profit from users and vendors alike by raising prices, utilizing deceptive practices ("dark patterns"), and otherwise abandoning their previous principles for a profit-at-all-costs approach.

Amazon, which drew users with impossibly cheap goods and free and fast shipping (built on the back of a global logistics empire rife with dangerous and dehumanizing working conditions), then jacked up fees for sellers and incentivized them to bid against each other for preference in its search rankings, at the expense of the user experience.

Google, which drew users with its revolutionary search engine, brokered exclusivity deals to lock in the dominance of its search—then intentionally lowered its search quality so users would spend more time (looking through ads) trying to find the information they were looking for, and then *further* lowered its search quality by disrupting its own model with misleading, incomplete, or plain incorrect "AI Overviews."

With few alternatives able to survive competition with these platforms, users and vendors are forced to tolerate the steadily degrading quality that defines enshittification, until they finally have enough and choose to leave, even at personal cost—causing the platform and the value that it once created to collapse.

If you've ever felt that despite our expectations to the contrary, the products and platforms we interact with have in fact gotten *worse*, enshittification is a simple, powerful explanation for how and why this experience now seems so ubiquitous in our modern world.

Is it so surprising that it happened with workplace diversity, equity, and inclusion as well?

A quick history lesson: in the United States, the humble origin of workplace DEI emerged as a means of regulatory compliance. The landmark Civil Rights Act of 1964 outlawed discrimination on the basis of race, color, religion, sex, and nation of origin and created the Equal Employment Opportunity Commission (EEOC), a regulatory body to enforce antidiscrimination laws.

The threat of EEOC lawsuits and penalties gave birth to what we now call diversity, equity, and inclusion work, primarily in the form of equal employment opportunity (EEO) training as a means of compliance—whether as a court-ordered remedy following a successful lawsuit alleging discriminatory practices, or as a proactive means to prevent the aforementioned lawsuits. These early trainings, mostly focused on recitations of the law and "do's and don'ts" related to avoiding discrimination, delivered little impact. By 1970, the number of charges filed to the

EEOC only continued to rise, while rates of employment discrimination and pay disparities stayed constant.[2]

EEO training was not the primary driver of positive progress during this time. That distinction fell to affirmative action programs, which sought to bring employment levels of demographic minorities up to become roughly proportional with their respective share of the local and qualified workforce. In other words, if women made up roughly 40 percent of the available qualified labor pool for a business, an affirmative action program would mandate that the business make a good-faith effort to work toward 40 percent women in its own employed workforce.

Affirmative action programs meaningfully made a difference in closing employment gaps and reducing hiring discrimination. As proof, federal contractors, who were required to abide by these mandates, desegregated far more quickly than noncontractor businesses did.[3] Their positive impact proved surprisingly hardy: in the 1980s, when the Reagan administration defanged the EEOC by reducing its budget, restricting its ability to enforce antidiscrimination laws, and stripping away its independent power, compliance-related training largely went away—but gains from affirmative action programs, even after regulation evaporated, *continued to multiply*.[4]

Why? Because regulation-mandated affirmative action induced businesses to make semipermanent changes in how they hired employees. They developed smarter screening processes. They built stronger referral networks. Even when deregulated, these investments in greater fairness continued to deliver strong returns, as well as positive progress toward desegregation, over time.

The deregulation of the 1980s, however, nevertheless had an enormous effect on how workplaces pursued DEI and other prosocial initiatives over the following half century. For one thing, formal affirmative action programs largely vanished as soon as they were no longer mandated. But as employers of this era would soon find out, in the vacuum left by government deregulation, customers, clients, employees, and the public at large felt increasingly anxious about the potential for corporate abuse and discrimination. They had every right to be anxious, given scandals ranging from Bernie Madoff's Ponzi scheme to the Love Canal environmental disaster to the Lockheed bribery scandal.

Deregulation may have allowed employers far greater freedom to pursue profit and operate with impunity. But it was employer-driven "self-regulation" that emerged as a parallel solution for resolving societal anxiety, skepticism, and criticism, while protecting employers' ability to operate how they pleased.

The logic was simple. If people's concerns about employers' social and environmental impact, labor practices, and ethical behavior are *liabilities*, but their concerns are limited by the *information* they have access to regarding employers' operations, then employers can profit by *manipulating and influencing* information to build a prosocial reputation without meaningfully changing their underlying behaviors or operations.

In other words: everyone is hungry to support organizations that actually walk the talk when it comes to human rights, social responsibility, sustainability, ethical behavior, and diversity, equity, and inclusion. But with little information on how a given business *actually* operates, we tend to rely on what businesses publicly signal. We assume that products that have "green" language on their packaging are more environmentally friendly than products that don't. We assume that businesses that release annual DEI reports and have DEI statements on their websites are less discriminatory than businesses that don't.

Rather than investing huge amounts of time, energy, and money into ending discrimination, for example, the logic of "self-regulation" instead drove businesses to invest a minuscule percentage of those resources into public relations campaigns, strategic partnerships with NGOs and public figures, corporate lobbying, and court settlements to keep victims of discrimination from sharing their stories and build an "antidiscrimination" reputation completely separate from their actual operations.

It was within this age of self-regulation, as business demand for reputation building disconnected from business operations exploded, that the diversity industry truly came to life. Fueled by a focus on employee and management training, workplace DEI programs proliferated across every sector and industry in the United States in many different forms. As I wrote in *DEI Deconstructed*:

> Some training sessions were days long; others were an hour or less. Some training used newer techniques informed by research; some used the methods most familiar to their seasoned facilitators. . . . Others relied solely on the facilitator's imagination. A few characteristics stayed constant across these new types of training: They were voluntarily requested from organizations and corporations rather than required by any external source. They focused on the experience of the training itself, the input, rather than the outcome of training or the impact over time. And they trusted implicitly that the more companies applied themselves to DEI, the more inclusive and equitable they were guaranteed to become.[5]

This optimistic assumption was broadly incorrect. A 2006 meta-analysis looking into the impacts of thirty years of diversity initiatives within over 700 workplaces found that the most popular approaches to workplace DEI were ironically the least effective.[6] Diversity training—whether unconscious bias training, diversity management, business case approaches, "colorblind" approaches, multicultural approaches, or experiential learning—almost universally fell flat, failing to create conclusive positive change in representation or employee thriving, and in some cases even making inequality *worse*.

Oftentimes, those deploying these trainings are completely oblivious to their actual effectiveness. Research from Gallup conducted in 2022 found that 85 percent of companies had training on recognizing unconscious bias, and that human resources (HR) leaders were optimistic about their success: a near-unanimous 97 percent of HR leaders agreed that "their organizations create real change" with regard to diversity, equity, inclusion, and belonging. Just 37 percent of their organizations' employees agreed.[7]

The gulf between leaders' naive aspirations and the sobering reality extends far further. According to a massive research study examining trends in hiring discrimination over time in six Western countries, rates of racial discrimination against Black, Asian, and Latino or Hispanic people remained high and constant in the twenty-five years between 1990 and 2015, with no signs of improvement, while rates of discrimination against Middle Eastern/North African people measurably increased.[8] In 1990, a non-White applicant would have to apply to 50 percent more positions to receive the same amount of callbacks as a White applicant. In 2015, despite the rise of antidiscrimination laws, business policies to increase diversity, and shifts in societal attitudes away from explicit racism, that same non-White applicant would have no better experience than in 1990.

Discrimination, in which workers are treated adversely based on protected characteristics like race, gender, religion, disability, or age, collectively costs American workers billions in lost wages and opportunities each year. For a single woman, over a forty-year career, the lifetime loss in wages due to gender discrimination ranges from $300,000 to over $1 million depending on the state a woman lives in and her race. A study by the Urban Institute and ProPublica over twenty-four years found that 56 percent of workers over fifty are pushed out of their jobs, with only 2 percent able to recover their careers.[9] Discrimination explains a sizable chunk of the growing wage gap between White and Black workers since 2000,[10] disadvantages American workers without a college degree,[11] and results in a staggering pay gap for disabled workers, who earn 42 percent less than their nondisabled coworkers—roughly $13,000 less on average each year.[12] The total proportion of American workers who experience workplace discrimination? Ninety-one percent.[13]

As wage disparities and discrimination rates stagnated, the DEI industry, or the loose federation of consultancies, vendors, and professional organizations that offer services or engage in partnerships requested by employers, exploded. Globally, workplace DEI is set to reach $15 billion in worldwide expenditures by 2026 and is projected to hit $27 billion by 2030.

Many of my more optimistic colleagues point to these numbers as a sign that workplace DEI will someday triumph, even despite its enduring ineffectiveness. I see this optimism as similar to that of people who assert that, eventually, Facebook and Amazon and Google and TikTok and Airbnb will make so much money that they will realize their mistakes and pass on some of those benefits to consumers just like in the good ol' days—that is to say, misplaced.

The reason DEI investment *has not* correlated with actual social progress or improvement, despite the enduring demand for positive change and social progress, is precisely because far too many organizations have enshittified their DEI. Too many employers have chosen to prioritize short-term reputational benefits by manipulating people's perceptions of reality rather than putting in the real work to improve that reality, to the detriment of employees, job seekers, and ultimately their organization's health and reputation. I've seen it firsthand.

I have seen employers, rather than taking decisive action to disincentivize and eliminate unfairness in a promotions process, bring in external workshop facilitators to teach women and racialized employees to "get better at self-advocacy."

I have seen employers, rather than building fair hiring processes that actually eliminate discrimination, simply add a boilerplate "pro-diversity" statement to their hiring portals. (Research has found that reading these kinds of aspirational diversity statements in the hiring process *reduces* employees' sympathy for victims of discrimination and actually *increases* job applicants' likelihood of being discriminated against.[14])

I have seen employers, rather than actually resourcing internal diversity, equity, and inclusion work with budgets or headcount, proudly delegate this work to burned-out, volunteer-organized employee resource groups (ERGs) to do this work for free.

I have seen employers, rather than actually solving internal problems with their workforce, hire a disempowered, underresourced Chief Diversity Officer or similar professional as a figurehead to stave off criticism, only to blame them when progress fails to materialize and sacrifice them for political points when facing external scrutiny.

These realities are depressing, but they aren't inevitable. Whether with DEI, tech platforms, sustainability, health care, or any other domain that has experienced enshittification, their decline may *feel* inevitable because we often feel like hostages of the employers and systems we have come to depend on. We continue to celebrate pro-diversity messaging because we have no other ways to gauge real progress, and we continue to cling to diversity reports noting marginal representational progress ("We increased our proportion of Black employees by 0.7 percent this year!") because we receive no other metrics. As workers, we continue to seek out ineffective diversity training and event programming because we have no faith that we will receive anything more; as DEI practitioners, we continue to provide ineffective diversity training and event programming because we need to earn a living, and tell ourselves that "something is better than nothing."

But none of this is inevitable. Doctorow, the writer who coined the term, has clear prescriptions for ending the enshittification of tech platforms: competition, regulation, self-help, and labor. Might these solutions apply as well to workplace DEI? You damn well bet they can.

The Path Forward to Real Progress

First, competition. The more employers and brands that DEI-conscious consumers and workers have to choose from, the more punishing it will become for employers to treat DEI as a performance rather than a reality. Brands that can differentiate themselves in a sea of enshittified DEI will win, and that differentiation comes not simply from better communication but from *actual progress*. The status quo of most DEI efforts today is to talk ad nauseam about "commitment to inclusion" or "valuing diversity" but to share next to no information about actual impact. Imagine the advantage conferred to those employers that measurably prove their achievement of fairness, inclusion, access, and representation for everyone, and bring their impressive communications apparatuses to bear on that genuine impact.

Second, regulation. The more employers fear that the financial or reputational repercussions from regulators will outweigh the gains from exploitation or misbehavior, the less emboldened they will be to misbehave. Increased regulation can help tamp down on employers' options for taking advantage of consumers or workers and cut through the noise of talk without action. California's law requiring gender quotas for corporate boards didn't concern itself in the slightest with whether a board of directors posted on social media during Women's History Month, but it did meaningfully reduce the number of all-male boards and measurably improve firm value, shareholder returns, and operating performance while it was at it.[15]

Third, self-help. The more options consumers and workers have for meeting their DEI-related needs beyond the brands and employers that hold us hostage, the less appealing employers' half-baked DEI efforts appear. Sure, ERGs might create community and shared purpose—but so too might a faith community, a sport or hobby, a grassroots organizing group, and other community groups outside of work. The more of these options that exist, the less pressure workers will feel to "bring their full selves to work" for an employer that is happy to exploit their DEI volunteerism but will have no qualms about laying them off anyway.

Fourth, labor. The machinery of any employer runs not on some visionary, profit-seeking executive, but on the dozens, hundreds, or thousands of workers that lend their labor to these efforts. Every self-serving DEI report is written by workers. Every reputation-laundering external partnership is agreed upon and executed by workers. Every ineffective sixty-minute unconscious bias training is sought out and delivered by workers. The more workers and professionals of all kinds can recognize that *our labor* allows enshittified workplace DEI efforts to continue, the more we can exert influence over those efforts to ensure they deliver real impact, rather than exploitation and broken promises.

I'll add one final recommendation to Doctorow's list of prescriptions: trust. One of the most damaging consequences of enshittification is something that we can all feel but rarely see: the loss of trust between an organization's leaders and its workers, external partners, customers, and even shareholders. It's this loss of trust that marks the invisible death spiral for organizations, and far too many leaders fail to recognize it until it's too late. American retailer Target, previously known for its strong reputation as a champion of DEI, made headlines in the early days of the second Trump presidency in 2025 by eliminating DEI-related hiring goals, ending racial justice executive committees, and discontinuing supplier diversity commitments. Progressive shoppers, feeling wholly betrayed by Target's actions, boycotted the retailer to great effect—foot traffic in its stores dropped for more than ten consecutive weeks and its stock prices nosedived.[16]

Only when employers successfully regain the trust between their leadership and constituencies, along the way restoring the unspoken social contract between them all built on value creation rather than value extraction, can they "dis-enshittify" their DEI efforts and escape their doom spirals.

Even with a clear prescription, turning this ship around will not be easy. Even the FAIR Framework, which I designed specifically to help those committed to the shared vision of a more fair, accessible, inclusive, and representative world push past enshittification to achieve these outcomes in reality, hits some but not all of Doctorow's recommendations.

The FAIR Framework is a powerful tool for employers to differentiate themselves and successfully compete with peers who have stagnated on their legacy DEI initiatives and communications. It presents clear actions that not only decision-makers and executives but also DEI professionals, everyday employees, and even conscious consumers can take to achieve real impact by rejecting poorly designed, performative . . . and yes, *enshittified* DEI efforts. It articulates a path forward for how all of us can rebuild the trust that was lost over decades of failed DEI efforts, even in a time of extreme backlash and polarization, by reimagining legacy DEI into FAIR work that is focused on results, fixes systems at scale, is driven by coalitions across our differences, and is motivated by a vision of creating greater abundance for all of us.

But what of regulation, the means by which governments can influence prosocial behavior by disincentivizing abuse and exploitation? Or self-help, the project of disentangling workplaces from our lives, so that we rely less on our employers as the sole providers of community and purpose (to say nothing of health care or basic survival needs as well)? That work lies beyond what any workplace-focused framework, whether

DEI or FAIR, can achieve on its own. That work requires our collective organizing as a people to shift our society toward a better future where everyone receives the dignity, respect, and opportunity we deserve regardless of the beliefs, values, needs, circumstances, experiences, and perspectives we hold.

What FAIR allows us to do is to transform employers from perpetrators of a stagnant and harmful status quo into entities that at minimum do no harm—and at best, can serve as allies in the work of building a better world for all of us.

It starts with the recognition that our best intentions are not enough to prevent unintended outcomes that might make problems worse: cobra effects. It starts with identifying how well-intentioned leaders and workers can rationalize short-term decisions that extract value, rather than create it, for those we initially work to benefit: enshittification.

With this understanding in hand, we can now use what we've learned to address anti-DEI backlash in our workplaces and communities. By creating real value and solving real problems, rather than walking in circles with ineffective workplace DEI, we not only resist backlash but fundamentally transform it—turning skeptics and critics from "enemies of the movement" into allies that might help us more effectively achieve wins for all of us.

2

TRANSFORMING
THE BACKLASH

On September 29, 2023, Claudine Gay was inaugurated as the thirtieth president of Harvard University, simultaneously becoming the first Black person and the second woman to hold the esteemed position in the Ivy League university's 386-year history. On January 2, 2024, she announced her resignation after a relentless and coordinated campaign leveraging conservative activists, billionaire donors, right-wing politicians, and unwitting news outlets made her departure all but assured.

Christopher Rufo, a conservative activist who has proudly described himself as a primary architect behind the campaign, was happy to brag about the tactics he deployed throughout the campaign. In December 2023, he tweeted that "we launched the Claudine Gay plagiarism story from the Right. The next step is to smuggle it into the media apparatus of the Left, legitimizing the narrative to center-left actors who have the power to topple her. Then squeeze."[1]

Speaking to *Politico* a month later, Rufo elaborated on his tactics. "I've run the same playbook on critical race theory, on gender ideology, on DEI bureaucracy. For the time being, given the structure of our institutions, this is a universal strategy that can be applied by the right to most issues," he shared.

"What I'm doing is teaching conservatives how to hack that system and to use our asymmetrical disadvantages to our strategic advantage. We need to be very lightweight and very aggressive, and we need to be faster and smarter and rhetorically more sophisticated than our opponents—who, unfortunately for them, have grown complacent, lazy, entitled and ripe for disruption."[2]

There's nothing particularly brilliant about the playbook that Rufo and other leaders of the anti-DEI movement use. Their core strategy is almost painfully simple:

1. Pick a target, whether a person (e.g., Claudine Gay), entity (e.g., the Department of Education), or program (e.g., a mentorship program for supporting women of color).

2. Prepare a political football in advance, crafting takedowns, talking points, and smear tactics that cast the target in the worst possible light and associate it with the most politically toxic affiliations imaginable (e.g., antisemitism, corruption, antimeritocracy, nepotism, communism, and so on) without regard for truth or accuracy.

3. Wait, vigilantly and patiently, for the target to make a misstep—whether for weeks, months, or even years—or ideally, engineer a misstep by leveraging social, financial, and political pressure.

4. When the moment finally presents itself, pounce. Flood every possible news outlet and information source with the pre-prepared talking points, repeating conjecture or even plain slander as fact. Insist that the ideas are being shared in good faith (they are not) to maximize the number of people repeating, debating, and eventually legitimizing these points, and pile on enough pressure that the target makes further mistakes, invites closer scrutiny, and ultimately is taken down.

The targets of right-wing backlash are highly predictable: racialized people, women, LGBTQ+ people, immigrants, and other members of socially marginalized groups in positions of power, and any institution that purports to actively support members of these groups. But rather than convincing everyday people to put on the white hoods and take out the pitchforks, today's right-wing extremists use populist language that validates people's existing fears and anxieties, prescribing a seductive solution: if only we had less DEI, if only fewer resources went to *them*, then perhaps things might get better for *you*.

I know this because I have interacted with people who repeat similar rhetoric within nearly every organization I have worked with in the last few years.

They dismiss DEI-related events as "wokeism" and accuse DEI itself of "reverse racism" or "reverse sexism." They insinuate that pursuing diversity, equity, and inclusion is equivalent to abandoning meritocracy. They imply that any attempt to change the status quo could only make things worse for people like them.

As recently as 2022, most people engaged in the day-to-day work of workplace DEI tended to dismiss these kinds of criticisms. They would say things like, "Some people aren't worth convincing" or "They're not the low-hanging fruit we need to focus on."

Now, in this time of backlash, people engaged in workplace DEI are scared of this same criticism. They say things like, "We can't give them any reason to go after us" or "They're too emboldened to say anything they want, and they know it."

This fear is exactly the point. Christopher Rufo, the conservative activist behind many high-profile anti-DEI campaigns, said as much when he boasted of his goal to "demoralize and derange my opponents."

But *both* right-wing extremists and workplace DEI practitioners are wrong about what gives backlash its power and how enduring it might be. Anti-DEI activists who characterize backlash as some "grand awakening" of social conservatism are incorrect—as I noted in the introduction to this book, *82 percent* of Americans support DEI-related statements. DEI practitioners who characterize backlash as a groundswell of hatred and prejudice are also incorrect—only 20 percent of people directly experience benefits from DEI, with the majority of people sharing that workplace DEI has no impact at all on them; some proportion of those people are bound to resent workplace DEI for that lack of benefit.

When I've *actually talked* to those repeating anti-DEI talking points, what they share tends to be personal experiences that are a far cry from either stubborn ideology or vitriolic hate.

One person shared with me that his manager had mistreated nearly every member of her team, but got away with it without repercussions by misusing the language of DEI to characterize herself as the victim; to him, workplace DEI was just another way for awful leaders to weasel out of accountability.

One person shared with me that her executive team had enthusiastically rebranded their organization as "committed to DEI" but was entirely dependent on exploiting the labor of their employee resource groups to promote their new brand; to her, workplace DEI was a cynical PR ploy devoid of actual benefit.

One person shared with me that the predominantly progressive culture of his workplace made him afraid to share even work-related differences in opinion, after being openly mocked by his colleagues for suggesting a different strategy to engage with a client; to him, workplace DEI was heavy-handed ideological conformity.

They didn't oppose workplace DEI because they felt it was "evil," even if the language they parroted from anti-DEI activists might have implied it. They opposed workplace DEI because their direct experience with it had been more negative than positive, plain and simple.

What these stories suggest to me is that anti-DEI backlash is neither a moral shortcoming to be squashed out of existence nor an unstoppable force of nature: it's the logical result of workplace DEI executed to less than its full potential. Bluntly put, if every one of the 82 percent of Americans that support pro-DEI statements *felt genuine benefit from workplace DEI*, backlash would be virtually nonexistent and anti-DEI activists would be taken about as seriously as Flat Earth activists.

This enormous gap between support and experience represents the enormous *opportunity* we have to do better. Anti-DEI backlash is just one marker of dissonance, feedback that the status quo of workplace DEI leaves liabilities that can be easily exploited by a small minority of opportunistic right-wing extremists. Recall that step 3 of the anti-DEI activist playbook is to "wait for the target to make a misstep": if workplace DEI is their target, they have so many examples to exploit that they need not wait long.

The solution to backlash is the exact same solution to "de-enshittify" workplace DEI: reimagine the work from the ground up to ensure it actually benefits everyone. Shore up its weaknesses, place positive results and real impact over the false comfort of feel-good messaging and conformity, reject the polarization of "left" and "right" to focus instead on closing the gap between "up" and "down," and involve *everyone* in the work to do better.

Sowing Backlash, One Training at a Time

Between 2015 and 2025, my nonpractitioner friends and colleagues probably shared with me something like twenty or thirty horror stories about DEI efforts occurring in their own organizations. (I'd like to think that they were asking for my advice, but more often than not it was conveyed in the form of lighthearted ribbing.)

There was the self-advertised "disability guru" with no experience working with disabled communities and no expertise applying accessibility standards, offering unsolicited advice to a product team over the protests of a disabled specialist who worked on that team. There was the "antiracism" speaker who bizarrely referenced long-discredited ideas from *racial phrenology* (yes, the 1800s-era pseudoscience purporting to categorize racial groups by the shape of people's skulls) to argue that racial differences were inevitable and absolute.

I heard stories about White men asked to identify and apologize for their own "White supremacy characteristics," about events highlighting expectations for women's unpaid labor in the workplace ironically organized by the unpaid labor of a women's ERG, about facilitated conversations ending in ugly shouting matches about "which group was the most oppressed," and about workshops that were indistinguishable from live therapy sessions for the facilitator at the expense of their captive audience.

Each one of these stories was shared with an apologetic cringe, as if my friends were telling me, "You can't seriously believe that doing this kind of nonsense actually makes workplaces better, can you?"

"Not at all," I responded every time. "But would you believe me if I said that this is the only thing workplace leaders will pay for?"

In chapter 1, I wrote about the employer shift that occurred in the 1980s from using DEI-related regulation to develop healthier organizational practices toward using DEI-related training to cheaply give the *impression of progress*. It was this shift that enabled enough enduring demand to fuel an entire DEI industry to meet it, after all. But because the benefit they seek is reputational gains and public signaling, they will naturally gravitate toward the shortest path to those goals available to them.

There are plenty of workplace DEI practitioners with no qualms about meeting this demand. Their business models revolve around their ability to provide easy, off-the-shelf services that promise maximum impact with minimal investment, a perfect complement for what employers request. Enshittified demand, meet enshittified supply.

While performative employers and performative practitioners fall into a symbiotic relationship with each other, *both* groups develop a parasitic relationship with the workers they "serve." Ironically, the people who lose most are the marginalized workers and customers whose experiences of marginalization and inequality inspired the work to begin at all, but who see little to no benefit from the endless reputation-burnishing events so endemic to workplace DEI.[3]

For decades, leading practitioners sought to prevent, slow, then finally undo this dynamic once it had been firmly established. The release of the first DEI-focused ISO standard, for example, was one high-profile effort to resist the "capture" of workplace DEI through standardizing what effective practices looked like.[4] But everything changed drastically in the summer of 2020, following the murder of George Floyd, a Black man, by a White police officer in Minneapolis.

Protests surged across the United States and in over sixty other countries around the world, as anger over persistent anti-Black racism, police brutality, and injustice boiled over. Almost overnight, it became apparent to employers and DEI practitioners alike that the cultural zeitgeist had fundamentally shifted. Workers in every industry and sector wanted their employers to acknowledge and take action on ending anti-Black racism, not only within their own workplaces but in society at large. Customers demanded to see indications that the brands they supported were demonstrably committed to the cause. Investors and shareholders increasingly saw a DEI strategy as a positive sign of an organization's financial prospects.[5]

The demand for expediency fundamentally reshaped the landscape of workplace DEI as employer demand for fast and flashy DEI training multiplied by a factor of ten overnight. Three months after the murder of George Floyd in 2020, job listings for DEI roles surged by 123 percent.[6] Chief Diversity Officer positions were swiftly created and filled, voluntary ERGs, diversity committees, and task forces proliferated within workplaces, and DEI professionals were suddenly inundated with hundreds of requests for training after training after training.

To many of my colleagues in the industry, some of whom were just about ready to close up shop and pivot their careers, the explosive rise in demand was bewildering, even exhilarating. Some rode the boom to rapidly scale up their businesses. Others quit their day jobs and went into workplace DEI training full-time. I still remember how one of my acquaintances described the post-George Floyd DEI boom as if a drought had broken and the rain had come.

At the time, it felt to me more like the toilet was overflowing.

Of the hundreds of weekly requests from business leaders that poured into my inbox during this time, a solid three-quarters were almost insultingly naive about the services they requested and the impact demanded.

"We would like to request a sixty-minute lecture on antiracism delivered within the next two weeks to help affirm our commitment to ending racism," from a desperate startup CEO.

"We would like to request a ninety-minute workshop on antiracism delivered within the next three weeks to help support our transformation into an antiracist organization," from a desperate HR executive.

"We would like to request thirty minutes of your time in the next week to help one of our clients craft a social media post about antiracism," from a desperate PR agency.

"Could you just come in and do an assessment of our organization? Our leaders only have eyes for workshops, so they're not paying, but we can draw from our yearly budget for you. Is $100 enough?" from a desperate ERG leader.

When I responded to each request asking for more information—about whether there were long-term plans, how leaders would follow up on the services requested, how they intended to measure impact and hold themselves accountable—*more than 90 percent of my emails went without a response.*

The intent behind these requests couldn't have been more obvious: workplace leaders, panicking over how to respond to the largest racial justice movement since the civil rights movement in the 1960s, were looking to enlist DEI practitioners in appeasing their restless workforce. The same leaders who had mercilessly laid off their internal DEI practitioners at the start of the COVID-19 pandemic were now begging for these same people to return so that they might serve as the face for employers' "commitment to antiracism" that they were woefully unprepared to do on their own.

Many practitioners refused to say yes to these requests. But enough *did* that employers got exactly what they wanted: a tidal wave of new enshittification in the form of on-demand, flashy "antiracism trainings" and similar check-the-box activities that could delay the ire of socially conscious workers, give cover to workplace leaders unwilling to actually change their organizations, and simultaneously buttress the reputation of socially conscious brands with the legitimacy of an independent practitioner.

My issue isn't that practitioners profited from the DEI boom in the wake of George Floyd's murder. It's that the most visible form of workplace DEI requested by employers and legitimized by practitioners during this time, the stand-alone sixty-minute DEI training, is perhaps the single most harmful intervention that could have been associated with workplace DEI. Its ascendancy as the "unit" of most organizations' DEI programs doomed these programs to failure from the start, and sowed the seeds of the very backlash we see today.

Imagine you were encouraged by your doctor to seek out a medical procedure that promised to improve your quality of life. And yet, in a review of nearly a *thousand* scientific studies on the procedure, numerous researchers found that the quality of life for those who had undergone the procedure was no different from that of people who had chosen not to.[7] Other researchers found that depending on how the procedure is undertaken, patients *might* see benefits for a few days—but any gains would dissipate soon afterward.[8] The most optimistic of these researchers argued that the procedure might be ineffective on its own but might result in some tangible benefits when paired with three additional procedures. Still other researchers found that undergoing the procedure might make your quality of life *worse*. The doctors explaining this to you wave aside this criticism with a smile. "The research might be mixed, but we think it's important to be open-minded. Would you consider it?"

If I had this information and heard that request, I'd be looking for the nearest authority to report malpractice.

This is the sobering reality behind DEI training, the poster child of today's thoroughly enshittified workplace DEI: despite its overwhelming prescription in organizations across industry and sector, in study after study, researchers find that it changes neither people's behaviors nor organizations' realities for the better.

At best, it leaves attendees no better off than those who don't attend or it creates lingering benefits that fade in days. At worst, it strengthens stereotypes about marginalized groups,[9] reduces empathy in people with at least one socially "privileged" identity (that is to say, most people),[10] worsens demographic tensions between groups,[11] exacerbates conscious and unconscious bias,[12] increases people's willingness to engage in discriminatory behavior,[13] and even results in lower demographic diversity in leadership over time.[14]

Having observed, participated in, and even facilitated some of these workshops in my own work, I'm inclined to agree with the research. One-off DEI trainings fail all who attend them. For people possessing historically marginalized identities, these trainings are far too short and limited in scope to truly solve any enduring organizational problems, and foster resentment and distrust toward organizations. For people possessing historically privileged identities (a group that overlaps heavily with the first), the blame-and-shame approach of these trainings routinely activates threat, resentment, and frustration, or gives them the false confidence that having taken the workshop immunizes them from possibly engaging in discrimination—which, of course, makes them *more likely to engage in discrimination.*

Post-workshop, members of this second group often feel like they have to walk on eggshells, like their identities make them "less valuable" than their coworkers, and like their possession of the "wrong" identities makes them deserving of shame. These negative emotions need to go somewhere, and the workshop facilitators have long since collected their paychecks and left. Instead, they direct their hostility in the form of backlash and increased discrimination toward the women, people of color, and LGBTQ+ people in their organization. Ironically, the most popular DEI effort for so many workplaces has the well-documented cobra effect of sabotaging the effectiveness of workplace DEI.

We Already Know What Works

In the same way that we now have nearly a thousand studies showing us the perils of solving workplace DEI problems with training, it turns out that we have scores upon scores of research and case studies showing us exactly what works instead.

We know that utilizing data analytics to measure the *results* of our efforts (rather than only tracking our inputs or good intentions), sharing this information transparently, and tying this measurement to internal and external accountability meaningfully changes people's behavior.[15]

We know that approaching this work as change management to shift the workplace *environment*—the systems, formal and informal rules, incentives, policies, processes, and practices that make up "business as usual"—rather than trying to change people's deeply held internal beliefs, works to change behavior at scale.[16]

We know that strategies that bring people *together* beyond their limited social cliques into larger coalitions and networks, as opposed to pursuing change through siloed, segregated, or separated efforts, work to build shared commitment and prevent intergroup tensions.[17]

We know that framing change work as creating greater abundance for all, rather than using adversarial, blame-and-shame, or zero-sum framings that imply progress for one group as necessarily disadvantaging another, works to defuse threat and mitigate backlash.[18]

These are the four tenets of the FAIR Framework: outcomes over good intentions, environment over individual, coalitions over cliques, and abundance over scarcity.

And yet, leader after leader continues to throw DEI training at the problem, fail to measure the impact of their initiatives, and ignore the need to change their workplace environment. DEI practitioner after practitioner continues to try and change people's biases in sixty minutes, pursue identity-related DEI efforts in silos, and focus on assigning blame for inequality and exclusion over creating shared responsibility for fixing it.

It's like watching a sink overflow onto the kitchen floor while simultaneously seeing the homeowners scratch their heads from across the house, wondering aloud how many more rooms they have to set on fire to successfully solve the problem.

Take the example of a workplace I worked with many years ago that, after assessing its employee engagement and retention, found a stark but puzzling gender divide. Women were highly engaged, decently happy, but heavily disadvantaged in promotion rates, pay, and leadership representation. On the other hand, men were undeniably overrepresented in leadership and advantaged in pay and promotion, yet they were disengaged and miserable, with a median wellness score far below that of women.

The organization had pursued the usual avenues but found them lacking. Forming a women's ERG helped enable the occasional volunteer-organized event, but hadn't solved the problems women faced in representation, promotions, and pay. Offering more wellness perks hadn't solved the wellness deficit experienced by men, nor their overall engagement. Bringing in a DEI speaker to lead an hour-long workshop on gender bias in promotions had resulted in an informative session that was attended primarily by women, but without workplace leaders (or many men in general) in attendance, with additional events focusing on mentorship, decision-making, and allyship not faring any better. If anything, the events were noticeably inflaming gender-related tensions. Women saw men's lack of attendance as an indication that bias, mentorship, decision-making, and allyship were not priorities for men, and as a confirmation that gender inequities stemmed from (male) leaders' lack of consideration. Men saw the content focus of these events as an indication that their negative experiences as men didn't matter and as a confirmation that men were seen as "the problem" despite their disproportionately poor wellness and engagement. In private conversations, women argued that benefits for women would come only when men gave up their power, while men argued that benefits for men would come only when women opened up more conversations to men.

The classic trajectory had manifested. Employees overwhelmingly saw event programming as the key battleground of the issue, despite the lack of efficacy these events seemed to have. Organizing an ERG, hosting events, and offering wellness perks were implemented because these initiatives were common and popular, but they hadn't been designed to solve any given problem or meet any given need and so hadn't achieved impact.

Workplace groups of men and women, both pushing for change, focused more on convincing others to agree with their interpretation rather than on building coalitions aligned against shared problems. Each group saw their issues as the most important, and communicated as if it were impossible for their own group to "win" without the other group "losing" something equivalent.

To solve these problems, I worked with this organization's leadership and passionate employee advocates to get curious about the root of their shared issues. What could explain women's higher engagement and well-being, but lower access to opportunity, pay, and success? What could explain men's abysmal well-being and engagement but stronger markers of career success?

In this workplace, it turned out the primary driver was overwork.

A culture of overwork established by those at the top, male executives with spouses able to manage household, childcare, and family responsibilities, created impossible expectations for what it meant to succeed in the organization. Employees who could regularly work more than sixty hours a week, respond to emails at midnight every night, and be on call to jump into work-related tasks were handsomely rewarded for their sacrifice. At the same time, while the organization had flexibility and remote work policies, these policies were framed as "accommodations" and heavily feminized: it was widely understood that any man taking advantage of these policies was committing "career suicide," while paternalistically, it was expected and encouraged for women to do so.

This dynamic created a two-tiered workforce. Senior managers and leadership teams were composed almost entirely of overworked men who had little time for nonwork activities and who lionized their self-sacrifice to cope with the demands of their jobs, while the entry-to-middle level of the organization was composed of women with far more flexibility and "work-life balance," but next to no long-term career prospects.

Any woman who aimed for senior or leadership positions was held to an expectation of productivity that was impossible to meet without overwork, and faced a prevalent attitude among decision-makers that "women weren't as prepared for leadership"—primarily because they couldn't make the sacrifice to work sixty-hour weeks. Simultaneously, any man who explicitly sought greater wellness and balance faced concern from leaders over whether they were "committed enough to the company" and faced the potential of losing opportunities because of it.

To fix this problem, we needed to do far more than hold a handful of workshops.

Coordinating with curious and sympathetic executives, we started from the top by examining (with the intention of shattering) the illusion that overwork was any marker of skill or productivity. This took months of data analysis and employee interviews to help pull out what truly drove success in business terms if not overwork. For this organization, it was possessing the emotional intelligence to build and maintain strong relationships; the management chops to coordinate teams, protect psychological safety, and insulate direct reports from politics; and the core operational expertise to ensure that organizational processes stayed functional even without direct supervision.

Executives weren't entirely convinced to abandon their overwork norms with that information alone, because overwork wasn't just functional—it was a status marker, something that brought them together and gave them a sense of purpose and meaning at the top. Even if it was no longer productive to be overworking, they wouldn't let those norms go without replacing them with something equivalent.

So we focused on building alternative rituals that they could adopt to build purpose and meaning in their roles, without necessitating 3 a.m. emails.

We piloted a new practice of having executives and senior managers celebrate "smart wins" instead of "hard sacrifices," sharing stories in weekly check-ins about how creativity and ingenuity led them to create value by working smarter, not longer hours. For example, when one manager solved a client problem that normally would take two weeks in just four days, we shared her story widely as a positive example of effective leadership. Simultaneously, we took steps to normalize the recognition that life happens and that workers have families, personal lives, and needs *outside of work* that are important to them—like encouraging leaders to share and learn about what matters to their team members outside of work. We spoke to a man who had defied the norm against taking parental leave to spend time with his family after the birth of his first child, and helped defend his assertion that doing so was so good for his wellness, sense of purpose, and commitment that he was more productive after returning to work than he had been before.

There were concrete practices we insisted on as well, like getting executives to use the Schedule Send feature on their email to ensure emails went out at 8 a.m. the next day, instead of at midnight, and communicating to all employees that they had a "right to disconnect" and ignore nonemergency work emails or calls outside of specific working hours agreed upon by everyone. Once those efforts saw success and built momentum, we also undertook an ambitious initiative to update formal evaluation and promotion criteria to better reward productivity and problem-solving—rather than just busyness and likability in the eyes of senior leadership.

One of the primary focuses of this work, undertaken over more than a year, was to build and engage a broad coalition of people with something to gain by transforming their organization for the better. It didn't look like an "activist movement," but we did engage activists. It didn't look like a "directive from leadership," but we did engage leaders. By focusing on the material benefits of building a better organization for everyone—career growth, wellness, purpose, access to opportunity, and more—and using our understanding of the environment to design targeted initiatives, we were able to build a broad tent of people who were willing to work toward the win-win, and stop backlash before it even started.

Years later, when I was brought back to help them interpret their latest employee survey data, I was proud to see their progress. Not all of their problems of overwork had been solved, to be clear, and they had far more work to do. But they had reduced many of their gender disparities by more than half. Men were far more likely to take time off and utilize flexible work benefits, and their wellness and engagement had increased. Women were more likely to be managers and senior managers, and their average time between promotions was approaching that of men. The ironic thing is that we had made enormous strides in resolving gender disparity but had hardly ever talked about gender. We had achieved enormous DEI progress but had hardly used the playbook of legacy DEI.

This is the kind of reset and reimagining of workplace DEI that can beat both DEI enshittification and anti-DEI backlash alike, a common-sense approach defined by tangible outcomes, working-environment changes, broad coalitions, and win-win framing, rather than by the performative words, self-help-focused initiatives, narrow cliques, and zero-sum rhetoric too many of our legacy DEI efforts have decayed into.

This approach is what I call FAIR, standing for Fairness, Access, Inclusion, and Representation. When we pursue the universal outcomes of fairness, access, inclusion, and representation for *everyone*, utilizing strategies that empower, engage, value, and learn from *everyone*, we can make it so that everyone wins.

We can get unstuck from our current stagnant progress and solve real problems impacting real people, creating better workplaces, better services, better experiences, and a better impact on the world.

By ensuring that the 82 percent who believe in the value of a more diverse, equitable, and inclusive world *actually perceive value* from our efforts to get there, we can stop backlash in its tracks. We can take the wind out of the sails of anti-DEI activists who rely on fear, threat, and scarcity to power their movements, simply by delivering so much confidence, safety, and abundance for all that the warped vision right-wing extremists present holds no appeal compared to the new normal we've built.

That's the vision. In the next chapters, I'll take a deep dive into just what it means to achieve it. I'll focus on each component of FAIR work, how that work differs from legacy DEI, and the specific practices that any practitioner or advocate can use to begin carrying out that work in their own organization to recenter on impact, defuse the backlash, and re-enable real progress for everyone.

3

FAIRNESS IS ENVIRONMENTAL

FAIRNESS is when an environment has been designed to support all people in succeeding to their full potential, free from discrimination and systemic barriers.

In 2003, economists Marianne Bertrand and Sendhil Mullainathan conducted a field study, an experiment in the real world, to learn about the extent of racial discrimination in hiring. They meticulously crafted fake résumés to apply to help wanted ads in Boston and Chicago, with just one twist: while the résumés were identical in experience listed, half of them were given White-sounding names like Emily Walsh and Greg Baker, while the other half were given Black-sounding names like Lakisha Washington and Jamal Jones. After applying to more than 1,300 help wanted ads with nearly 5,000 résumés, the researchers sat back and waited for the callbacks to come in, wondering if they would find a disparity between the callback rate for White-sounding résumés versus Black-sounding résumés.

They found disparities—enormous ones. If the résumés had belonged to real people, Lakisha and Jamal would have to apply to 50 percent more jobs just to get the same number of callbacks as Emily and Greg. When the economists analyzed the data to quantify this gap, they found that a Black job seeker had to have the equivalent of *eight more years of experience* to be considered "just" as qualified as a White job seeker, all else being equal.[1]

A similar study conducted a decade later, this time utilizing more than 6,000 online job applications for jobs in Arizona, found that the odds of getting a callback for a White candidate *with a felony conviction* were still higher than the odds of getting a callback for a Black candidate *with no conviction*.[2] Demonstrably, racism was very much alive and well.

When people learn about these studies, they usually come to similar conclusions: discrimination isn't fair, and qualified candidates shouldn't be overlooked simply because of their race. You'd be hard-pressed to find people who would argue that such a clear-cut and transparent example of discrimination could possibly be considered "fair." Where the conversation gets murkier, however, is when we ask what it might take to make this situation more fair for the candidates facing discrimination.

The common prescription in response to unfair outcomes, among both DEI practitioners and workplace leaders, is to implicate the *individuals* in the system for acting unfairly and seek to change those individuals' thinking and behavior.

"It's unacceptable for so many hiring managers to be biased against Lakisha and Jamal," they might conclude. "They must believe that White people are better than Black people, and that's unacceptable. We need to stamp out those biases until our hiring managers become unbiased people, so that they might act fairly."

This perspective argues that racism lives in the minds of racist people, who engage in racist behaviors that result in racialized people (in the United States, Black, Indigenous, Latine, Asian, and mixed-race people) being treated unfairly. To get to fairness, proponents of this argument make the case that we need to change the behaviors of racist people by eliminating their racist biases.

Straightforward, right? But there are a few problems with this line of thinking, chief among them being that the root causes of discrimination—racism, sexism, ableism, transphobia, homophobia, antisemitism, Islamophobia, wealth inequality, and so on—go far deeper than the isolated actions of a few bad apples. Scholars across the disciplines of public policy, sociology, political science, history, economics, and many others have identified that these issues are *systemic*—that is to say, so deeply embedded in and reproduced by the fabric of our society that they have become environmental constants.

Individual biases are the symptom of the problem, not the cause. It is no more possible to uproot racism or sexism by focusing on individual biases than it is possible to save a failing garden by uprooting diseased plants—when the soil has dangerous chemicals leaching into it, the rain is acidic from pollution, and the local wildlife feasts on whatever survives. As antiracism advocates often say, "Racism is the water, not the shark."

In the original example, Lakisha and Jamal résumés didn't face discrimination simply because the hiring managers who reviewed their applications were racially biased. Discrimination occurred because the employers of those managers lacked safeguards to prevent bias from turning into discrimination and lacked incentives and processes to drive fair behavior—even from people who may privately hold biased beliefs.

Fairness, the first word in the FAIR acronym, diverges from legacy DEI by focusing on the environment rather than the individual. Rather than attributing unfair outcomes to individuals' biased behaviors and beliefs, FAIR instead sees unfair outcomes as the result of poorly designed *environments*, which can be redesigned to achieve fairness even without fundamentally changing the people within them.

"It's unacceptable for so many employers to tolerate racial bias in decision-making," FAIR practitioners might conclude. "Their lack of safeguards, resources, and support for decision-makers shows a lack of responsibility over their outputs, and that's unacceptable. We need to build an environment that is fair by design, where decisions are made fairly regardless of the personal biases of individual decision-makers."

It's a subtle distinction, but a powerful one.

In the most recent iteration of the same kind of field study, economists at the University of California, Berkeley and the University of Chicago submitted a whopping 83,000 fake job applications for over 11,000 job openings. Not only did they find that, even twenty years after the first study, employers were *still* more likely to call back applicants with White-sounding names, but they also found that employers varied dramatically in how discriminatory they were toward the fake résumés.

Some firms in their study had virtually no racial discrimination at all, calling back Black applicants just about 3 percent less often compared to White applicants. Other firms were egregiously discriminatory, calling back Black applicants *24 percent less often* compared to White applicants.[3]

What explains this divide? The industry to which an employer belonged, as well as how centralized an employer's human resources departments and policies were. Standardized hiring processes that use hiring panels involving multiple people, structured interviewing practices, and hiring rubrics that clearly indicate the skills and experience valued in new hires can make decision-making more fair, regardless of the biases held by individuals within that process.[4]

Pat Kline, an economics professor involved in the study, said it well: "Individuals are inevitably going to carry biases along with them, [but] it's not automatic that those individual biases will translate into organizational biases."[5]

You might think that by sharing this information, I've turned a simple problem of solving individual bias into a complicated problem of making organizational change.

Surprisingly, it's just the opposite. Despite the explosion in the last few years of workshops and training purporting to change or eliminate individual biases, research shows that *none of them work* over the long term, and some even cause backlash that *worsens bias*,[6] because bias reinforced over a lifetime of interactions with biased educational systems, workplaces, media portrayals, and interpersonal relationships simply cannot be dispersed in one sixty-minute training, or even ten sixty-minute trainings. Imagine buying a fan—or ten fans, even—to improve your home's air quality while a wildfire tears through your neighborhood. It's just not happening.

Fairness by design, despite sounding more intimidating, is far more achievable. Not only do we have no shortage of evidence-based strategies for successfully mitigating bias, safeguarding fairness, and ending discrimination, but many of these strategies can be carried out by anyone— whether a leader, changemaker, or ordinary person. The thing is, many of these strategies don't look, sound, or feel like what people have come to expect from workplace DEI. They don't focus on changing people but on changing the environment. They don't compel behavior with mandates but influence it at scale with norms and incentives.

The practitioners I work with often debate the merits of this reframing with me. The most frequent pushback is their argument that, at a bare minimum, an individual focus doesn't have to be at odds with a systems focus. "Systems are made of people," they often share. "There's still a place for individual change, individual courage, and individual leadership."

I don't disagree entirely—but if the ratio they're hoping to hear from me is 50:50 in terms of focusing on systems versus individuals, they'll be disappointed. From my perspective, the ratio should be closer to 90:10.

Individual Activism Will Not Save Us

In late 2019, a number of my leadership consulting clients began sharing with me uncharacteristically dubious ideas for resolving inequality in their own organizations. One recruiting leader floated the idea of purposefully presenting a slate of candidates to hiring managers where every candidate had a disability. One manager excitedly talked about the possibility of creating all-female teams and how she might work with human resources to do so. A third leader casually shared his intention to sidestep his company's hiring process to bring his friends straight to the interview phase, in the name of increasing diversity.

Two of these leaders cited as the inspiration for these ideas a recent panel that a famous marketing executive, Bozoma Saint John, had participated in.

"If I want to increase the numbers of Black women in tech, I'm going to do it myself," Saint John declared during the panel, about her approach as an executive building a team. "As I looked through the résumés that were not 'diverse candidates,' I just started pulling from my group of friends... by the time the fourth [Black woman I had hired] came along, I got the call [from HR]. They were like, 'Is there any way we can help to make sure that we're looking at a broad range of candidates so that you have a broader pool of people to hire?' Did you tell [the White man] down the hall that? Did you tell him that he can't hire any more White men? Because I don't think so."[7]

Saint John's argument in this story is that her workplace's hiring process had never been fair for anyone, least of all for Black women. In the face of overwhelming inequality resulting from blatant nepotism as the law of the land, she chose to boldly use her influence to utilize those same tactics "for good," daring the powers that be to go after her and implicate themselves in the process.

It was clear that this story struck a chord with many leaders. I can't deny that it appealed to me as well.

I've seen hiring managers brag about looking up the addresses of job applicants to easily discard résumés from people living in poor neighborhoods. I've seen sexism in all its forms, from justifying the withholding of a promotion from a woman because she had children, to discriminating against a male applicant for a role in a female-dominated sector, to offering technical and constructive feedback to men but useless and "nice" feedback to women, to creating perverse incentives for men to overwork regardless of their desire for work-life balance. I've had surreal arguments with employers blatantly looking for loopholes to avoid complying with the Americans with Disabilities Act.

It's tempting, in the face of a clearly rigged game, to do a little rigging yourself if you can.

Unfortunately, most of us don't command the same kind of celebrity—and perhaps invulnerability—as Bozoma Saint John. For the rest of us, attempting to solve unfairness and inequality by fiat is likely to incur unintended adverse consequences, both for us and for the people our actions affect.

As I told the leaders I worked with, if they circumvented the formal hiring process to bring in candidates of their choosing, even for noble reasons or even if other leaders committed similar abuses, they would be single-handedly sabotaging those candidates' careers. The label of "diversity hire" is a sticky and pernicious one, and once applied, it relentlessly undermines affected workers. Research shows that employees hired either explicitly or implicitly because of their social identities—*regardless of their actual qualifications*—are likely to face extreme resentment, perceptions of lower competence, and attempts by their colleagues to restrict their influence.[8] They are likely to experience shame from their entry into the organization, experience self-doubt, and even develop stigmatized self-perceptions of lower competence.[9]

As for the well-intentioned leaders choosing to implement these kinds of strategies? In the United States, they risk accusations of engaging in illegal hiring discrimination in violation of Title VII of the Civil Rights Act of 1964, and risk scrutiny and punishment from not only their HR departments but also their organizations' general counsels. In the UK and other countries in Europe, this behavior would be considered "positive discrimination" and risk similar scrutiny and punishment. It was imperative that I steer the leaders I worked with away from those strategies.

While these examples are high profile, they are motivated by the same focus on individual activism and individual advocacy that drives much of legacy DEI work. Practitioners and leaders alike share feel-good narratives that suggest *anyone* can become a hero and make a difference on their own. Individuals can single-handedly stop discrimination if they "speak up"; they can single-handedly fix hiring inequality by "becoming unbiased"; they can single-handedly create belonging and safety by "protecting their colleagues." The driving assumption is that by building individual skill, knowledge, and courage, any individual can change even the most enduring and complex workplace environments and prevent even the worst embodiments of discrimination and unfairness through their own abilities.

I bought into the same narrative myself earlier in my career. Working for a technology company, I helped design, facilitate, and follow up on what I believed to be a best-in-class training aimed at increasing bystander intervention: the ability of individuals to speak up and challenge discrimination when they witnessed it, contributing to a feedback-friendly culture in their workplace. It was a one-time, two-hour training—but in the moment, it felt magical. Attendees practiced speaking up in facilitated scenarios. They made plans for resolving barriers to bystander intervention. They were confident that, moving forward, the small slights and discriminatory incidents that characterized their workplace would no longer go unaddressed.

One year after the first training, I had the rare opportunity to deliver a follow-up session for the same client. Many of the same employees from the first session showed up at the second, and so I got to excitedly ask the question many workshop facilitators dream about: "What changed as a result of the workshop I delivered?"

An awkward silence fell over the room.

"Not much, unfortunately," one person shared. "You did a great job, and we learned a lot of skills! But few of our managers make it safe enough to speak up. We wanted to use our skills, but we didn't want to lose our jobs."

I had delivered a fan, but I hadn't put out the fire. I had given individuals the false confidence that they could change the system on their own, but hadn't done anything to remove the environmental blockers—unsupportive managers and a culture of conflict aversion—that kept the same patterns locked into place. Now, the million-dollar question: Why had the company been more than willing to pay for my labor to develop and deliver the training, but done next to nothing to invest in changing their environment so that it could succeed?

Optimistic practitioners might chime in by saying, "They just didn't do enough. It's not enough just to pay for individual-focused training. They also have to pay for systemic change."

These days, I'm not convinced by that argument. Did you know that some of the largest corporate manufacturers are also the largest lobbyists and promoters of individual recycling initiatives? By shifting the conversation to what individuals can do to "be a part of the solution," they obscure the reality that their own businesses are the primary contributors to the problem. This gives them cover to continue operating with impunity by churning out more and more single-use plastics each year, 80 percent of which are never recycled. This waste clogs up landfills, forms floating islands in our oceans, and breaks down into microplastics that make it into our bodies and get passed down to our children.[10] But by all means, more of us need to put more plastic bottles in the right bins.

I find it hard to believe that employers have naively made the same mistakes around their workplace DEI efforts for decades, and that continuing to nudge them to "pay for real change, not just performative initiatives!" will compel any real change. They're paying for individual-focused training precisely because it gives them cover to *not* pay for systemic change.

How We Unrig the Game

Many of our organizations are rife with discrimination, exclusion, and unfairness, not because of a few bad apples, but as the stable output of a toxic environment. Climbing the corporate ladder until you have the invulnerability to do whatever you want isn't a strategy that most of us can use. Using harmful tactics "for good" incurs extreme risk for ourselves and the people we try to help. Designing strategies that attempt to fix people rather than fix their environment either falls short, creates surface-level change that fades quickly, or activates backlash that makes the problem worse—but remains the most in-demand service employers are willing to pay for and, accordingly, the service that workplace DEI practitioners are most willing to provide.

But it's quite possible to unrig the game if we focus our efforts on the workplace environment rather than on the individuals within it. Reviving a previous metaphor: if our garden is getting decimated by poisoned soil, acid rain, and opportunistic predators, then we can save it by both changing the environment and shielding the garden from harms we can't change. If we transplant our crops into healthier and well-fertilized soil, protect them from acid rain by watering with filtered or spring water, and put up fencing and natural deterrents to protect them from predators, and if in the meantime we invest in cleaning the polluted air and soil, then eventually our garden will flourish.

Building fair organizations takes the same approach, just with different outcomes. When people assess their own experience of fairness in the workplace, the outcomes they typically think about include the following:

- Total compensation
- Hiring

- Promotion
- Managerial support
- Learning and development
- Feedback and evaluation
- Discipline and conduct
- Termination and job changes

In other words, people want to be hired, paid, promoted, supported, developed, given feedback, held accountable, and if necessary, disciplined fairly—without discrimination or favoritism. The aspirational goal is true organizational fairness: where the only inequalities that exist are those that result from people's *choices and performance*, because systemic barriers like discrimination have been removed and because guardrails and resources have been added throughout the workplace that ensure fair treatment for all. If people have more, it's because they chose to pursue more, achieved more, and were rewarded with more—not because they were well-liked, played the right politics, or simply experienced less discrimination than their colleagues. (There's another name for this aspirational end state: "meritocracy.")

Achieving fairness, far from insisting that everyone experience the exact same outcomes, is about insisting that everyone experience the same *high standard of support* regardless of their individual needs. People want to be treated fairly when being hired, regardless of their gender or race. They want to be treated, paid, and promoted fairly, regardless of their disability or accommodation needs. They want the same high standard of managerial support, feedback, and opportunities, regardless of their faith, sexuality, or family status. They want to be treated fairly when facing discipline or termination, regardless of their age.

How do we change our working environments to achieve this vision in a way that centers outcomes over intentions, environments over individuals, coalitions over cliques, and abundance over scarcity?

In my own work, I use the following seven-step process:

Understand → Rally → Design → Involve → Experiment → Incentivize → Celebrate

This work starts with identifying the presence of unfairness. Rather than relying only on hearsay, conduct demographic analyses on the workplace outcomes we identified to uncover disparities—just like the economists conducting field experiments on résumé callbacks.

For any given outcome, say "average time between promotions," collect data on both social demographics (race, gender, disability, age, religion, sexuality, parental status, and so on) and organizational demographics (manager, tenure, department, seniority, etc.). You may opt to examine all of this information at once, especially if you have access to some or all of it through an existing database like a human resources information system (HRIS), or to collect the most salient demographics through optional surveys that ask respondents to self-identify with their demographics. Be sure to follow data collection best practices to protect anonymity and confidentiality whenever collecting demographic data, and be careful who you share this data with. (The line separating a well-intentioned HR professional asking, "I wonder who shared this feedback?" and a workplace retaliation suit is thinner than you think. Don't test it.)

What you're looking for are key disparities that can't be explained by coincidence or factors outside your organization's control. For example, say that your analysis reveals that women in your organization tend to spend a disproportionate amount of time on office housework, running errands, taking meeting notes, organizing meetings, and so on. Furthermore, they tend to be assigned project roles that are highly important but less explicitly valued by the organization's leadership ("team player" versus "rockstar" roles), and as a result, it takes longer on average for a woman to rack up the kind of experience that leaders find to be promotion material. Perhaps due to both the presence of gendered beliefs regarding the kinds of work women are "more suited" for, and the lack of strong processes that create fairness at scale, you might conclude from this analysis that women face unfair obstacles to a fair promotion experience compared to men—and that to improve fairness, you should focus on addressing gender inequality. **Understand? Check.**

Leaders tend to rush into problem-solving as soon as they have an understanding of an issue. Rushing, however, runs the risk of backlash. Even if it's entirely true that your workplace's promotions process is unfair to women compared to men, simply announcing this as justification for overhauling your promotions process and then diving into changemaking is likely to rankle men and result in their disengagement from, resistance to, or even outright sabotage of your efforts. Why?

Research on backlash to diversity, equity, and inclusion work finds that there are three major drivers of backlash to change: the perception that one's social group will *lose out* on resources, the perception that one will be *unfamiliar with or excluded by* new social norms, and the perception that one's social group will be *demonized* as the source of the problem.[11] It's closely linked to a psychological phenomenon called loss aversion—describing the common human reaction of responding more strongly to any potential loss (of resources, respect, stability, security, you name it) than to an equivalent potential gain.

This is where storytelling comes in as a critical tool to rally your workforce around change well before you implement any change initiative. A well-communicated narrative not only builds momentum and excitement around the need to improve upon the status quo but also explicitly counters each major driver of backlash.

You might work closely with men to identify and communicate *benefits* and *gains* related to resource availability following the change; for example, a fairer promotions process might result in more gains for men who perform well, regardless of their background. You might stress that many valuable social norms aren't changing (such as the importance of relationship building and communication) while explicitly noting the collective benefits of adapting to the social norms that *will* change (such as a reduced likelihood of managers operating entirely in silos, and greater accountability from other leaders). Finally, you might intentionally communicate the value of future opportunity, rather than pointing fingers of blame for past unfairness, to defuse feelings of potential threat or exclusion.

Done right, you're able to galvanize members of your workforce across role, title, and social identity to feel energized and hopeful about the benefits of change for everyone, even if they may have directly benefited from the previous status quo. **Rally? Check.**

Even with a clear-eyed understanding of your own workplace and the backing of a motivated workforce, it can still be easy to design an ineffective solution. Which of the infinite numbers of levers you can pull will create real change rather than cobra effects? Change management scholarship offers insights.

In a famous story often shared with students of social psychology, anthropologist Margaret Mead and organizational psychologist Kurt Lewin jointly led a project to increase the household consumption of hearts, liver, and other organ meats in response to food shortages during World War II. How do you think they did it? Patriotic jingles? Eye-catching pictures of tripe? Lectures on the nutritional value of liver? The answer is both insightful and utterly mundane: they targeted the food-related beliefs of housewives.

At the time, housewives were the major decision-makers when it came to what food to put on the table. But organ meats were broadly associated with food that "other people" (namely, poorer people) ate. By facilitating discussions among small groups of housewives to build a perception of organ meats as food that "people like us" eat, framing an ask as something relatively small ("Introduce organ meats for variety, once in a while"), creating a space for members to share their own concerns and problem-solve together, and then, of course, sharing cooking tips for making organ meats taste delicious, these small-group interventions had an enormous effect. National organ meat consumption rose by *one-third*.[12]

What the Lewinian school of change management teaches us is that making change doesn't have to require pushing hard, just pushing *smart*. If you understand the environment well enough, you might be able to identify opportunities for major impact with only minor adjustments. (Other times, a close analysis may reveal that the only path forward is to make a major change. In this situation, don't hesitate to go big either!)

Bringing in a small but focused team of experts, each with a strong understanding of the environment and the issue, allows you to strike the right balance between deep insight and speedy iteration. The best solutions speak directly to the root causes behind the problems they seek to solve and are tailored heavily for the context they are deployed in. Once you have a pilot and a strong rationale for why you believe it'll work, you're ready to move on. **Design? Check.**

Using the promotions example, say you choose to focus on changing the behavior of your direct managers, because they have the largest influence over the assignment of high-profile projects. Should you send them an email asking them to become more fair, *or else*? Sure, if you want them to despise you.

No one likes being told what to do, especially if they have a vested interest in maintaining the behaviors they are told to change. In some cases, resistance against the threat of change can be so strong that people double down on the original behavior—a phenomenon called the Romeo and Juliet effect. (I hesitate to describe the relationship between managers and their ineffective habits as "star-crossed lovers," but sometimes it does feel that way, yes.) This particular finding is a common one in research on backlash against workplace DEI: managers, facing insinuations that their discretions enabled inequality and discrimination, rebel by taking even more discretion and discriminating *more*.[13]

So don't tell your managers what to do; work *with* them to figure out a plan. By working directly with those who have something to gain (or lose) from your intervention, understanding their concerns, and integrating their feedback into the intervention design, you can help people feel a greater sense of ownership over the intervention and develop a personal drive to see it succeed. By better meeting their needs than the status quo does, and by reducing the barriers present in the status quo, you can transform managers from reluctant partners or irate targets for change into enthusiastic collaborators.

Say your managers express needs for autonomy and respect, and have long clashed with their partners in human resources—whose bureaucratic expectations and back-and-forth bog down managers' autonomy and make them feel disrespected when making promotion recommendations. Say you develop standardized criteria and clear guidelines for what makes a person ready for promotion and use these new materials to accelerate decisions within promotion committees. Everyone gets what they want, and everyone feels like they've won. **Involve? Check.**

Only at this point do you put your solution into practice, after doing everything you can to set it up for success. Start small, with a pilot deployed only within a team or department. Keep an open mind and prepare yourself to collect good data and honest feedback on how successfully your pilot solved the problem—or not. *Data is accountability, not a pat on the back.* Be mindful of what questions you ask to make sure that you're learning about your solution's actual impact, rather than just collecting vanity metrics that make you feel good. A workshop might score 4.9 out of 5 stars on "participant satisfaction" and still utterly fail to reduce discrimination—and if you ask only about the former and not the latter, you might convince yourself your workshop delivers "data-driven success." Yeah, not so much.

Instead, measure the outcomes that most directly capture the problem you're solving, the behavior you're hoping to drive with your solutions, and potential cobra effects you might have anticipated during the design phase. If you rolled out a new promotions process to improve fairness and reduce gender inequality, then measure the gender distribution of newly promoted managers before versus after the change. Survey all decision-makers who participated in the new process, asking them to indicate their thoughts on how the new process compares to the previous process in terms of fairness, respect, autonomy, and speed.

Your intervention will almost certainly be less than perfect the first time around. Understanding where it has room to improve, or if it was even the right intervention in the first place, can help you focus your efforts. Good data allows you to keep the lines of communication open between you and the partners you worked with to design and collect feedback on your solution, and to redesign your solution as many times as needed to ensure it works. **Experiment? Check.**

As your effort grows more and more effective through increasing rounds of feedback and iteration, you'll begin scaling it from a small pilot into a legitimate organizational change initiative. But as your reach expands, you'll increasingly be asking people to participate in new processes and practices that they know nothing about and had little hand in creating. Everything has to get bigger to accommodate. The narrative you've developed has to turn from an email blurb into a firm-wide communications strategy. The team of experts and leaders you've put together has to turn from a scrappy working group into a bona fide movement and organization-wide coalition.

As the goals of your efforts get more ambitious, the tactics have to scale with them. No longer are you asking a handful of promotions committees to try a new process; instead, you are setting the expectation that *every* promotions committee utilize the new process. Relying on good intentions and passion can only get your change initiative so far. Like the first stage of a booster rocket falling to Earth after liftoff, to keep the momentum going and *institutionalize* change, you'll need to utilize the tools of the organization to incentivize continued adoption and participation.

Praise and recognition are powerful tools that both leaders and ordinary people can use to accelerate the pace of change. By recognizing those pushing the adoption of the new solution and rewarding them with informal (yet still valuable) praise, you can signal to others in the organization what behaviors matter. An executive might explicitly call out and praise the leader of a department that successfully adopts the new promotions process, holding up their achievement as the example to follow. Expectation setting and accountability help to recast change as the "new normal," even when done subtly. Adding a line in the job description of HR practitioners and managers pertaining to their stewardship of the fair promotions process, for example, can drive home the idea that the new fair-promotions process is here to stay. **Incentivize? Check.**

At the very end of the process is success: the achievement of real progress toward fairness for all by removing barriers and creating a more effective organization for everyone. This final step looks in many ways like the first several. With data collected from across the organization, you conduct one final analysis to prove that your efforts have had the effect you intended. Did you actually make the organization more fair for women by mitigating inequality in the promotions process? (Ideally, if you've been keeping an eye on this throughout your efforts, you shouldn't find any major surprises. If you do, revisit previous steps and iterate until you find success.) If the answer is yes, then you're almost at the finish line. Utilizing the coalitions you've built across the organization, cap off the story you've been telling throughout the entire process by answering the following:

- What did you achieve?

- What did you learn?

- What contribution did each partner in the effort play?
- How does this strengthen your values and your purpose as an organization?

And then, after all that? *Throw the biggest party you can afford to throw.* It's mandatory. Celebrate, recognize, and reward everyone who contributed. Brag about it to your customers, to your stakeholders, and on social media. Celebrating your wins—when the wins are *real* and correspond to real value created for real people—helps close the loop of the changemaking process and convert those wins into sustainable reputational gains for your organization. It builds trust and goodwill between workers and leaders. It institutionalizes the change work that occurred as part of the organization's culture and history. And it locks in that change as the new standard of "business as usual," on top of which future changemaking efforts can build. **Celebrate? Check.**

It takes genuine commitment to move away from the deceptive simplicity of individual activism to the more rigorous, yet simultaneously *more achievable*, work of changing the environment of an organization for the better through our collective efforts. And yet, this is exactly what FAIR guides us to do to unrig the game—to beat backlash, rebuild trust, and build workplaces that are fair by design.

4

ACCESS IS GOOD DESIGN SANS DUCT TAPE

> ACCESS is when all people can fully participate and engage with an experience, environment, product, or service as a result of their access needs being met.

In the late 2010s, I began working with a large American university to help students better navigate the frustrating labyrinth of their internal information systems.

For students who were using a different name than the one they had submitted to the university upon enrollment, whether due to marriage, a legal name change, or even a preference for a nickname that wasn't their legal name, we developed a resource that helped guide them through a complicated series of steps that we had come by through trial and error. This process started with talking to *one specific* IT professional within the university who was sympathetic to the initiative and working with that professional to create an entirely new student profile with the new information.

We would then reach out to IT professionals across the complex constellation of student records and information systems throughout the university that might contain the old information, working to manually edit the ones that could be edited, delete those that couldn't so we could replace them with the new profiles, and ensure that all information was consistent across these systems. An entire Rube Goldberg machine of step-by-step patchwork fixes, all so that when professors pulled up information about a student in their class, that information would be up to date and help them communicate with the student in the way the student wished.

I remember once talking to a university staff member about this effort and receiving praise for it. "It's so good that you're giving an option for those students to feel affirmed as their authentic selves," the staff member said.

If I were dealing with a leaking roof by catching water in buckets, would they have praised me for "giving the rainwater an option to be of use"?

What we were providing was a duct-tape "solution" at best. There was simply no reason for these IT systems to be designed this poorly, and even if it was "good" that people like myself had created a workaround, that workaround was exhausting and frankly demeaning for students—who deserved the same quality of experience in their classrooms as their peers, without needing to go through these bureaucratic nightmares on the side.

Years later, long after I had stopped working with the university, I learned they had finally consolidated all of their old IT systems into a centralized system that allowed name changes as a matter of course, rolled out under an unassuming "nickname" update. Suddenly, a long-standing problem for married students, adopted students, transgender students, and any other student who was arbitrarily excluded by the old system was erased in an instant, and the patchwork fix that I had created, reliant on the charity of random IT professionals across the university, was made utterly obsolete. I couldn't have been more relieved.

Access, the second word of the FAIR acronym, is about ensuring that *everyone* can participate fully in the things we build, and achieving it requires that we fundamentally rethink our design and decision-making processes to put the needs of our audiences first, rather than last.

You may have heard about access before in the context of *accessibility*, the design of products, services, experiences, and environments to be usable by people with disabilities. These concepts are linked, but the way I define access as part of the FAIR Framework goes a little deeper. Within legacy DEI spaces, accessibility is discussed in almost insultingly uninspired terms. "Disabled people are part of your target audience, too!" reads one article. "Don't forget to add disability to your DEI program," advises another. "It's time to talk about disability," crows a third. Common across far too many of these articles, as well as in the workplace DEI programs I have seen over the past decade, is the perception that accessibility is simply a matter of advocating for the causes that disabled people and people with disabilities believe in, and that disability is simply one entry on a laundry list of identity issues present in an underpaid director of DEI's event programming responsibilities.

But to me, this view has always fundamentally misunderstood the guiding principle behind accessibility: that by reimagining the processes that decision-makers use to create the world around us, we can put people's needs *first* rather than last and design a world that truly works for everyone—without requiring post hoc accommodations or duct-tape solutions, like the one I helped develop for the university in the story I used to open this chapter.

This view of accessibility starts from disability but is powerful enough to apply across every dimension of difference. Disability, and also age. Also gender, race, sexuality, size, first language, parental status, and so on. Access needs are universal, and unfortunately, we have a long way to go before we achieve full participation from everyone.

Our world is full of soap dispensers that don't activate and self-driving cars that don't stop for people with darker skin,[1] personal protective equipment (PPE) that doesn't fit women or non-White men,[2] medication bottles that can't be opened by people who need to take medication, and websites and internet infrastructure that are inaccessible for people with disabilities—with only 3 percent of the internet considered accessible.[3]

Our workplaces are full of workplace offsites scheduled during non-Christian religious holidays, office thermostats set so low that women pile on blankets during the summer, facilities that are physically inaccessible for people with disabilities, and parental leave policies designed so poorly that LGBTQ+ parents rarely get the leave they need, whatever their gender.

Think about your workplace and the world around you, and ask yourself if you've ever felt the difference between being in a space that *recognizes and meets* your needs and being in a space where you have to *suppress* your needs to fit in.

Too many of our workplaces again and again find themselves building the latter and seeking greater access through duct-tape fixes and second-rate modifications. But so long as their standard process for making decisions and designing experiences, products, services, and environments puts users, customers, and employees last, the things they build will rarely align with people's actual needs.

Imagine that you had the job of ordering shirts for a group of people you didn't know, once a year. How would you go about the process?

If you aimed to be like most workplaces, then every year you'd simply order an inventory of just the shirt *you wanted*, in the size and style that fit you, and distribute it to the group. If people complained about their shirts not fitting, you would shrug your shoulders and direct them to talk to a coworker who reported to you, who had no authority to change your decisions but *did* have a pair of scissors to make scrappy modifications, a list of local tailors, and the ability to order one customized shirt at a time—though it would be expensive and of lower quality. Every year, you would bring in an inspirational speaker to talk about the importance of shirts fitting well, give a speech about your commitment to buying shirts that fit, and claim that next year's shirts would be better. When the next year rolled around, you would bulk order the shirt that you wanted once again and happily tune out the frustrated feedback you once again receive from the group. They'd just have to deal with it.

This is the relationship that far too many organizations have with achieving access at present: although they speak regularly about its importance, their business-as-usual decision-making and design processes are fundamentally opposed to ensuring access for all.

Legacy DEI efforts on their own rarely crack this paradigm. In fact, it's often DEI practitioners that take on the role of the coworker with the scissors or the inspirational speaker in the metaphor—serving as duct-tape solutions at best, or reputation laundering of the status quo at worst.

The FAIR Framework guides us to fundamentally rethink this paradigm. By repositioning the audiences of our decisions as *design partners* of this work, rather than passive consumers of it, we can design dramatically more accessible and beneficial solutions for all—and mitigate a huge chunk of the back-and-forth criticism, deflection, outrage, and appeasement that many organizations engage in with their customers, workers, and audiences. By regularly utilizing practices of inclusive and universal design in tandem (more about this later), we can meet the widest range of needs in the most effective possible ways—without the demeaning, time-consuming, and inefficient duct-tape "fixes" that define so much of our world.

If we revisit the metaphor of buying shirts, FAIR would have us start by talking to the members of the group before even thinking about making a purchase. We'd ask about shirt sizes, obviously, but also about more important things. What are their needs when it comes to a shirt that they won't just donate in a few months' time without wearing? Do they have any sensitivities or restrictions regarding materials? For that matter, is a shirt really what they need in the first place? By letting go of our own assumptions and personal preferences as decision-makers and instead seeking to meet the needs of the group however that might manifest, we set our decisions up for success from the start.

Jumping over the Missing Stair

Blogger Cliff Jerrison coined the metaphor of a "missing stair" in 2012 to describe the phenomenon where known abusers are allowed to continue participating and operating within a community while those around them, rather than directly addressing the issue, direct others to avoid the abusive person.[4] "[A missing stair is] something you're so used to working around, you never stop to ask 'what if we actually fixed this?' Eventually you take it for granted that working around this [abuser] is just a fact of life, and if he hurts someone, that's the fault of whoever didn't apply the workarounds correctly."

We can apply this metaphor more broadly, not just to individually abusive people, but to harmfully or poorly designed environments as well. Like the physical problem the missing-stair effect takes its name from, of choosing to teach everyone to jump over a missing stair instead of fixing the staircase, organizations are rife with these kinds of issues. HR departments might quietly choose to transfer people out of a toxic manager's department rather than hold the manager accountable. Leadership might respond to falling trust and growing cynicism by taking Q&A off the agenda after company town halls and announcements.

In these examples, we have to assume that at some point the stair "broke," and the organization refused to fix it. But in many cases, the staircase was built with a missing stair from the start because a decision-maker failed to design with the needs of the collective in mind.

Sasha Costanza-Chock writes in *Design Justice: Community-Led Practices to Build the Worlds We Need* that "designers tend to unconsciously default to imagined users whose experiences are similar to their own" and that the resulting products, services, experiences, and environments that emerge from these processes work for some but not nearly all.[5]

Like the planner who bought the shirt that they wanted and imposed that decision onto everyone else, many designers and decision-makers consciously or unconsciously use themselves as the template for their choices. This phenomenon has a name, *egocentric bias*, and it's one of the reasons why decisions and designs often miss the mark (and, interestingly enough, why new entrepreneurs so often make products no one wants[6]).

Trying to correct this self-centered bias by designing for the collective doesn't work well either. When we try to design for the statistical average of all people, we end up making something that doesn't truly work for any actual person (statisticians like to joke that if your head is in the oven, and your feet are in the freezer, on average you feel just fine). As Tom Hillegonds writes in an article on the website Thrive, "When you design for the average, you're designing something that will ultimately leave every single user unsatisfied in one way, and no one user satisfied in all (or most) ways."[7]

When we try to design for disparate "types" of people, we too often end up relying on our own misguided stereotypes about groups—to the point where we might make a decision or create a product that substantially offends or fails to meet the needs of our audience. For example, Dolce & Gabbana's 2018 ad depicting a Chinese model failing to eat Italian food with chopsticks was widely criticized as offensive to Chinese people.[8] And consumers are turning against the trend of "shrink it and pink it" in product design, referring to the lazy attempt to increase profits by selling women a superficially different, and often functionally lower-quality "gendered," version of a product.[9]

A common criticism, often from progressive audiences and advocates, is that "there must have been no people in the room from the community." The assumption is that the presence of a single woman could prevent a sexist decision, the presence of a single Black person could prevent a racist product, and so on. But the problem lies deeper. It's not just *who* makes decisions but *how* decisions are made that keeps us walking in circles with our needs perpetually unmet.

I see it all the time in my work with organizations.

A company built a new office with heavy doors that did not open automatically, without first consulting disabled employees or accessibility experts. When disabled employees raised concerns, HR was instructed to document the offices where those employees worked and contract with a third party to install aftermarket automatic door modifications for their offices and bathrooms on that floor. Every other room on that floor and in the office was inaccessible—and disabled employees were now functionally restricted from ever moving into another physical office. Meanwhile, in offices without those modifications, employees who hadn't disclosed their disabilities were now scared to, worried that irate HR representatives would take out their frustration on them rather than on business leaders. Some resorted to waiting outside office doors until a colleague passed by, while others attempted to push them open anyway, exacerbating their disabilities in the process.

In one workplace, employees working remotely could not join most company meetings due to IT challenges that had stretched on for weeks and months. Rather than dedicating resources to resolving the issue or finding other creative ways to engage hybrid and mostly remote employees, leadership instructed the employees to "find ways to show up at the office in person." Many of these employees had previously agreed-upon arrangements to be working from out of state. It took the threat of an ADA (Americans with Disabilities Act) lawsuit for leadership to begrudgingly fix their IT issues.

What we need to realize is while these examples may be egregious, these kinds of stories are neither rare nor surprising. Inaccessible experiences that necessitate duct-tape solutions are the *standard*, if not outright the intended goal, of decision-making processes that put the needs of users, consumers, and employees last, and are a common facet of millions of people's lives. As long as the processes that drive these decisions stay the same, the inaccessible outputs of those processes will, too. And as long as the inaccessible products, services, experiences, and environments stay the same, the common response of duct-tape solutions and jumping over missing stairs will, too.

Workplace DEI rarely solves these problems. If anything, it tends to get terminally stuck at the stage of talking about them. A colleague of mine once spoke about how his workplace hosted a high-profile panel on ableism and disability-related discrimination at work. Prefaced by a statement of commitment from their executives and DEI leaders, the panel they platformed shared raw and vulnerable stories from employees who had experienced mistreatment. Due to the huge outpouring of support, excitement, and attendance at the event, workplace leaders vowed to make it a tradition to host the panel every year—but crucially, forgot about the part where they needed to end the disability-related discrimination that necessitated it. Two years later, the panel had to be canceled. The lack of tangible change had finally used up the trust of disabled employees, who no longer wanted to share their stories on stage as "trauma porn" for executives and practitioners alike, who were perfectly willing to admire their problems but far less willing to actually fix them.

Disability advocates and activists tend to be the ones at the forefront, with or without the help of legacy DEI—according to one source, as of the late 2010s, only 4 percent of workplace DEI programs had a focus on disability.[10] These days, leading disability organizations are pushing for disability to be anywhere *but* DEI, citing the lack of substance, follow-through, and resourcing of legacy DEI efforts.[11] I don't find this shift surprising. No matter how well-intentioned or how charismatic the person leading it, a program focused on flavor-of-the-month event programming and Band-Aid solutions that provide cover for their organization's missing stairs can never make the kind of change those excluded by the status quo—disabled or otherwise—deserve.

If FAIR aims to do what legacy DEI could not, then it needs to do far more than fix access issues with duct tape and host events that highlight inequality without actually fixing it. The pillars of the FAIR Framework show us that effective change has to focus on results, tackle the root causes of hard problems, build coalitions of the many, and articulate the benefits for everyone. With access, that work starts from the curb.

The Power of Curb Cuts

Have you ever looked at a sidewalk and noticed the little ramps connecting the curbs to the street? Those are called curb cuts, and as much as we might take them for granted today, they came about in part because disabled veterans returned home to the United States after World War II only to find that public life wasn't easily accessible. Nearly fifty years of activism, disability rights movements, and the pioneering efforts of individual cities led to the ADA in 1990, which mandated that curb cuts be installed on all sidewalks.

Curb cuts make public life more accessible for people with disabilities. They also, as it turns out, help parents with strollers, people with temporary mobility issues, older adults, bikers, kids with toy wagons, people with luggage, delivery drivers with handcarts, joggers, skateboarders, and many more groups of people than I can name. You've almost certainly benefited from them, even if you haven't realized it until this moment. This is the most famous example of the eponymous curb-cut effect: the phenomenon where designing specifically for the needs of people with disabilities and other people experiencing marginalization, rather than some abstract "average" person, often results in unexpected benefits for far more groups than originally envisioned, and benefits to society at large.[12]

If you have taken an elevator, read subtitles or closed captions, used a single-stall restroom, or listened to audiobooks, you have benefited from accessibility via the curb-cut effect. Same goes if you have used an electric toothbrush, kitchen tools with extra-grippy handles, or drinking straws. Each of these inventions and innovations was created to improve the quality of life and preserve the autonomy and dignity of *people with disabilities*, and by doing so, they met so many other needs for so many other people that they have become fixtures of modern society. Many of us take them entirely for granted. It's nearly unthinkable today to imagine going back to a world without these innovations—a world with more barriers.

How did these inventions come to be? Did a brilliant designer or brilliant decision-maker see the potential to create a better world by learning about the needs of disabled people, and gamble on a new invention? No. For most, disabled people designed what others would not, fighting uphill the whole time. When it comes to curb cuts, disability activists based in Berkeley, California, against broad apathy and resistance to change from the general public, made the solution themselves by sledgehammering sidewalks, mixing their own concrete, and creating their own makeshift ramps in the dead of night.[13] As other changes, like wheelchair lifts on buses and lower countertops, began emerging, protests erupted nationwide, demanding that these accessible practices become the standard in all facilities—eventually leading to the passage of the ADA.

If you're a designer or a decision-maker, how might you best apply the insights from the curb-cut effect in your own organization or community? You might be told to look into approaches like *inclusive design* and *universal design*.

Both inclusive design and universal design are philosophies and methodologies for designing things to be usable and accessible for the largest number of people. They frequently exist in tandem and are slightly different in their prescriptions: whereas *inclusive* design looks for multiple solutions that meet multiple needs, *universal* design looks for a single solution that meets as many needs as possible.

Say you're seeking to ensure that people can participate fully in the experience and environment of an art museum. Inclusive design might mean ensuring that there are many *different* ways to experience the art and the museum based on people's needs. The art itself might be hanging on the wall, to be looked at and appreciated. But for people with visual impairment or low vision, there may also be braille descriptions, audio guides, or even tactile versions of the exhibits. Descriptions of each piece may be reproduced in multiple languages to reduce any language barriers preventing a patron from fully experiencing the art. Unique educational programs or guides might be available for patrons of different ages or for patrons with learning disabilities. Collectively, these solutions ensure that patrons have many options to meet their varied access needs.

For that same museum, universal design might mean ensuring that the *standard* experience in the museum meets as many people's needs as possible on its own. Perhaps the layout has been designed to minimize noise, harsh lighting, and crowd density to avoid sensory overstimulation. All text and signage have been presented in a large font, with good color contrast, and in clear, straightforward language. The physical space itself has been made accessible for people using mobility aids and designed to have many places to sit and rest. Together, well-applied inclusive design *and* universal design help ensure that all people can participate fully in the experience and environment you've created.

Here's the thing: neither inclusive design nor universal design is a philosophy that a designer or decision-maker can simply impose *upon* an audience and expect to achieve success. The lesson from the activist history behind the curb-cut effect is that the people with the most insight into the best possible experience, environment, product, or service are rarely the designers or decision-makers in charge of making them, and that decision-makers' attempts to design *for* an audience—rather than *alongside* them—often fall short.

You cannot successfully implement either inclusive design or universal design until you learn to let go of your own preconceptions and ego as a decision-maker or designer and welcome the influence of your audience to drive the process itself from the very start.

It's far easier said than done, for most of us. What would you do if you set out to solve a problem by organizing a gathering of people? You'd likely apply at least some of your own preferences for the gathering, like format, medium, length, and so on, and only later ask for feedback from those who might attend (if you ask for feedback at all). Even if you say that you're "open to changes," the likely reality is that much of what you've suggested is nonnegotiable by the time you've shared it, and everyone knows it. In fact, if someone were to suggest that the gathering *did not need to happen in the first place*, or *did not meet the needs of the audience*, you'd probably feel at least a twinge of annoyance. How dare they suggest scrapping all of your hard work! Why couldn't they be more sensitive and do their best to work with what you suggested instead?

Have you ever tried to help someone in your life, but rather than asking them directly what they're dealing with and what they might need, you instead made an assumption and followed through as if that assumption were a fact? If the person you're "helping" were to push back and tell you that your well-intentioned solution wasn't helpful, you might feel offended or even angry at them, especially if you put a large amount of effort into your "helpful solution." How dare they reject your kindness; you were only trying to help! Why couldn't they be more sensitive and do their best to work with what you suggested instead?

In both situations, you would have found yourself slipping into the familiar comfort of prioritizing your own beliefs and your own ego over the needs of the audience you were originally trying to help. We've all done this. Scrapping our own preconceived notions about what "help" might look like or what others' needs even are is hard—and yet it's exactly what we need to do if we want to achieve access and full participation from everyone in the things we make.

From the start, we have to *invite our audiences in* to let their needs drive our decisions. Building a consistent *process* that puts everyone's needs on the table, even if that means taking a different direction from the one we first envisioned, sets us up for the best chance of success. This is why disability advocates say "nothing about us without us,"[14] rather than "make sure there's braille." You can't cheat this step with stereotypes. If new mothers are part of your audience, you can't simply look up "best practices for including new mothers" and call that inclusive design.

Instead, seek input at every step of the way with an open mind. Remember, your design or decision is an evolving solution for a challenging problem or a deep need—not a reflection of your own ego or ambition.

List your prior beliefs about what the solution might look like, so you can be aware of what biases you bring to the table as a designer or decision-maker.

Take special care to select users outside the statistical "average" to complete surveys and interviews.

Test your prototypes and early drafts with others outside your immediate team to understand whether you're headed in the right direction and to get critical feedback.

Take the initiative to look up best practices, but when in doubt, if "best practice" says one thing and your own audience clearly needs something else, follow your audience.

Seek opportunities to find the curb cuts, rather than protect the missing stairs, and look to reflect in your decisions not just what individual people say they want, but what people truly *need*—so that you create solutions that work the first time, no duct tape required.

On an individual level, this shift in process is something that any decision-maker or designer can initiate immediately, though it'll take some practice. If you run meetings, you can choose to run them more accessibly. If you put on events, you can choose to organize them more accessibly.

But organizations as a whole becoming places where decisions and designs put audiences first, rather than last, is not a transition that happens overnight. Any leader trying to initiate change is likely to hit several brick walls: the inertia of the status quo, the comfort of jumping over missing stairs, the false efficiency of letting others patch up poor decisions with duct tape, and the simple fear that giving up control means courting failure.

The FAIR Framework offers guidance for overcoming those barriers.

I spoke once with a leadership team that had created such an abysmal company culture that their turnover rate was nearly 30 percent each year—forcing them to spend extravagant sums on constantly rehiring and retraining a revolving door of talent just to stay afloat. The team, however, was so deeply mired in their own poor habits that they saw this turnover rate as completely unrelated to their own leadership. "Not many people can handle our environment," one half bragged. Outside the leadership team, they didn't have a single employee who had been with the company for more than five years. Their terrible turnover rate, driven by their own dysfunctional management of their organization, was a missing stair they had convinced themselves they *enjoyed* jumping over.

To change the status quo, we have to first reveal just how much it costs. We have to translate the painful externalities of "business as usual"—the often unseen weight of the many small inefficiencies, injustices, and inaccessible experiences borne by those marginalized by poor decisions and designs—into language that leaders simply cannot ignore. The goal is to draw on the naked truth to make the status quo *intolerable*, to point at the missing stair and blurt out, "Why are we just jumping over this instead of fixing it?"

"Unless you change how you lead, you will run your business into the ground" is what I ended up telling these leaders. It took comparing their hiring and retraining costs to the industry average, connecting their leadership practices to other organizational issues that they already cared about, and working with them to identify their best and brightest workers who had been lost to the competition to drive this point home.

When people finally become open to changing how they make decisions and how they design experiences, it creates the best opportunity to fix missing stairs. But even enthusiastic leaders can only do so much to change a practice that has become normal and expected. If your organization has normalized spending two weeks designing an ad, two weeks gathering feedback on it, one month running the ad, and one month doing damage control and apologizing for it? It won't be easy to build an entirely new process, even if everyone involved hates how things are done.

If people tend to adopt new behaviors—or cling to old ones—not due to deeply held beliefs, or even rational self-interest, but simply because doing so feels easy, valuable, and normalized, then we can influence change if we can make it easier, more rewarding, and more normal to try something new, and harder, costlier, and weirder to stick with the old status quo.

If you want your organization to spend more time designing and gathering feedback on your ads so you can spend less time apologizing for them, consider ways to make that change feel easier, more rewarding, and more normal. Perhaps you might reallocate your budget to support more user research, or create formal and informal incentives for the best-made ads (that require minimal damage control). Perhaps you might make a big show of responding to a team that made a poorly performing ad, which in the past you would have overlooked, to make the point that the norms have shifted.

You can draw on what you know about your workplace to facilitate this process even more effectively.

Do your workers prioritize work that feels more fun and therefore rush through the design process into prototyping and iteration for that reason? Make reaching out and engaging with target audiences so fun that no one would willingly skip out on it.

Do your leaders prioritize decision-making processes that limit risk and therefore undercommunicate with groups seen as more likely to criticize decisions? Highlight the risks of *not* engaging with these groups, and make communicating feel as easy and safe as possible.

Throughout this entire strategy, sell the narrative of the curb-cut effect. In relentlessly positive terms, communicate how substantially a better process for making designs and decisions might benefit not only the specific groups marginalized by the status quo but also *everyone* in an organization or community. And don't just make this empty talk—keep an eye on what actually changes for the better, and talk up those wins when they materialize.

In the story I told at the beginning of this chapter, the university that finally consolidated its archaic information systems—dramatically taking the weight off married, adopted, and transgender students who had struggled through their name changes—was smart to not frame its update as an "adopted student accessibility initiative." They knew that an update framed this way would be ignored by virtually everyone. Instead, they highlighted the smoothness and interconnectedness of the new system for *everyone*, from students to teaching assistants to professors to IT professionals across the university, and spoke aspirationally about how these changes would make the classroom experience feel even more seamless for all.

It was a strange feeling, seeing the duct-tape solution disappear overnight, and seeing the missing stair that I and so many people had jumped over simply get fixed. For a short while, I felt a sense of loss over the fact that some of those hackneyed systems we had worked so hard to build no longer existed. But eventually, I realized that with the underlying access issue solved, everyone was better off than they had been before. The change had provided real value and solved real problems by bringing people together and highlighting the win-win for all. I could not imagine anyone opting to turn back the clock and return to a system with more barriers—which is precisely the revolutionary value of good design sans duct tape, as it provides greater access for all.

5

INCLUSION IS
SOLIDARITY AT SCALE

> INCLUSION is when all people feel valued, respected, physically
> safe, and psychologically safe for who they are, across all dimen-
> sions of difference.

A few years ago, I partnered with a Fortune 500 company to advise and
strategize with their internal network of employee resource groups, or
ERGs. Like many ERGs, the voluntary and employee-organized groups
within this company focused on building community for (usually one)
demographic identity or experience at a time, bringing people together
to talk about shared issues, celebrate shared culture, and provide mutual
support. In this company, they included a group focused on women;
groups focused on Black, Latino, Indigenous, and Asian American
communities; a group focused on disability; a group focused on the
LGBTQ+ community; and a group focused on parents.

On the surface, there was little about these groups that gave me
the impression they needed help from an external consultant. Many of
these groups regularly put on both smaller community events and larger
events for the entire organization. The larger events, particularly the
ones put on by the ERGs related to gender, race, and sexuality, were so

well attended that they had become cultural mainstays within the company, a point of pride that recruiters routinely showcased as evidence of their "commitment to inclusion" to attract top talent.

But things were not as rosy as they seemed from the outside.

As I spoke to each of the ERG leaders, I learned that they were barely treading water, caught between the expectations of their colleagues both inside and outside their own ERGs, and often feeling isolated from—if not in outright conflict with—their fellow ERG leaders. Within their ERG communities, leaders fielded daily comments to "do more." Members of their communities, strongly motivated by their desire to participate in advocacy and their own less-than-positive experiences navigating discrimination and exclusion, urged ERG leaders to push the organization toward greater change and at a faster pace. They were getting tired of celebrating their identities without making real progress in improving their actual experiences.

Their colleagues outside the ERGs, including executives, *loved* those celebrations. They saw them as palatable, two-dimensional representations of culture that they could safely sample without the discomfort of interrogating discrimination and exclusion. They were happy to clap for a lion dance performance and sample food at a South Asian food fair, but looked the other way when employees raised concerns about anti-Asian discrimination. They were happy to spotlight the stories of "inspirational" women in leadership who had persevered despite the barriers they faced, but twiddled their thumbs when it came to removing those barriers for other women.

As these tensions rose, the mood within the ERGs was turning them into pressure cookers. By the time I spoke to ERG leaders, many were talking about how "us versus them" was becoming the unspoken reality. A feud had erupted between the women's ERG and the Black ERG over dueling allegations of anti-Black racism in the women's ERG and sexism in the Black ERG. The LGBTQ+ ERG drew scrutiny when an event speaker, a White transgender woman, argued that "trans people are the single most oppressed group, period," as a reason for why their group should receive more funding. These leaders, facing critique from all sides and thanklessly churning out events despite it, were increasingly becoming burned out and disillusioned not only with their own ERGs but also with the entire project of workplace DEI.

To make matters worse, backlash was beginning to simmer across the organization as skeptical and cynical workers voiced claims that the company's focus on "marginalized communities" was itself marginalizing for straight, nondisabled White men. Despite the company's stated commitment to inclusion, these employees argued, its commitment only manifested in the form of events focusing on a select number of communities and social identities. "We deserve to be included too," they declared.

The executives I spoke to were at a loss. To them, inclusion was a low-risk investment in improving their company culture that had turned into yet another battleground of unresolvable conflict and a new minefield that was more trouble than it was worth. "I don't suppose you can help us get our ERGs back to where they were in 2015?" one asked, half desperately.

The answer was no. But as I made expressly clear to both executives and ERG leaders, there *was* a way forward for them if they had the courage and follow-through to transform their commitment to inclusion from a "feel-good performance of difference" into the genuine achievement of a workplace culture that worked for everyone, across every dimension of identity and difference.

This is what inclusion should always have been: the felt presence of value, respect, and safety for all people in an environment, across all dimensions of difference, achieved by organizing *across* our differences to bring people together, rather than organizing *against* our differences to split people apart.

Within FAIR, this is precisely how inclusion is redefined to be more accountable and measurable than its legacy DEI counterpart. When everyone, across all dimensions of identity and difference, feels valued, respected, and both physically and psychologically safe, then we have achieved inclusion. When you've led a meeting that achieves these standards, you've led an inclusive meeting. When you've built a team or a workplace where these standards are regularly achieved every day, you've built an inclusive team and an inclusive workplace. But so long as any person or group experiences the *absence* of value, respect, and safety—exclusion—then you have work to do.

Achieving this standard of inclusion for everyone, across all identities and differences, requires much more than a full event calendar. It's a simultaneous challenge to build a truly inclusive environment and a well-designed culture that makes space for our differences, keeps us focused on what we can do as a unified collective, and mitigates backlash by providing benefit to everyone—a challenge that, while difficult, should sound comfortingly familiar at this point. Mitigating backlash was the entire focus of chapter 2. Changing the environment was the entire focus of chapter 3. Good design was the entire focus of chapter 4.

By bringing these skills to bear, we can transform the minefields that so often manifest in identity-driven work into town squares where people can feel seen in their full humanity and collaborate all the better with each other as a result. We can solve the real problems that restrict people's full humanity and take away their sense of respect, value, and safety. We can create powerful shared norms that uphold an inclusive culture for everyone. And we can do it all collectively, through vibrant coalitions that tackle the messy work of organizational change and learning outside the silos that have come to predominate this work.

There are barriers in our way to achieving this vision, of course. There always are! Some of these barriers come from those who seek to uphold inequality at any cost, who act out of prejudice or superiority. But many of these barriers are self-imposed by DEI practitioners and social advocates, behaviors we adopted once upon a time to protect our peace that have turned into self-destructive habits that hold us back. Experienced social justice organizers and leaders have long put forward alternatives that can get us unstuck, if we only find the courage to pursue them—and they're practically revolutionary in their simplicity.

Canceling the Oppression Olympics

Maurice Mitchell, the national director of the Working Families Party and a visionary social movement strategist, is one of the foremost writers and thinkers in the work of movement building and progressive organizing. While I would like to directly quote the entirety of one of his brilliant essays, "Building Resilient Organizations," the essay itself is longer than any one chapter of this book—and so I instead will paraphrase his major insights.[1] More than any other resource cited in this book, if there is one thing you should put this book down to dive deeper into, let it be this. The lessons that took me nearly ten years of fumbling around in movement-building work to learn were crystallized by Mitchell in a piece that takes a mere ten minutes to read.

Mitchell, as a longtime organizer and strategist, has seen dozens of well-intentioned movements for positive change derailed by the same shortcomings over and over again. While his writing identifies many such shortcomings, the ones I will highlight here are *identity essentialism, maximalism,* and *glass houses/small wars.*

Identity essentialism, as Mitchell defines it, is when people "use one's identity or personal experience as a justification for a political position." Many of us have witnessed or perhaps participated in this rhetorical shortcut many times. To give our opinions or perspectives more power and legitimacy, especially in progressive circles, we tack on a blatant appeal to our social identities. Saying "I think this organization is a good one" comes across as simply a matter of opinion. Saying "As a person of color, I think this organization is a good one" comes across differently— as if I am both insinuating that they are a good organization *because they are good to people of color* and suggesting that *other people of color ought to agree with me.*

This rhetorical shortcut is very easily abused. A few years ago, I found myself locked in an argument with a colleague over the effectiveness of a given communication strategy for a client we were both working with. (The actual strategy in question wasn't even relevant to our debate— something about corporate values in action.) My colleague, rather than focusing on the substance of the debate, was fixated on the nature of our disagreement itself. "As a queer, disabled woman," she kept repeating, "the strategy will do harm."

I couldn't understand what she was trying to say. The strategy had little to do with any of the groups she had named, and yet she continued repeating her comment like it was a talisman against my disagreement.

Eventually, tired of arguing in circles, I snapped at her.

"As a *queer, neurodivergent, trans, nonbinary person of color,*" I said while rolling my eyes, "I think this strategy will work. Can you please listen to what I'm saying about why I think so?"

All of a sudden, she grew very quiet. "I didn't know all that about you," she mumbled, and immediately conceded the argument. I stared at her, bewildered. The productive debate I was hoping for evaporated in an instant, as if instead of talking through our ideas she had demanded we participate in some avian dominance ritual to determine pecking order, and I had fluffed up my chest bigger than she had. In my exasperation, I had done the equivalent of accidentally entering the arena, stumbling onto the field, and winning a silver medal at the Oppression Olympics. It didn't feel great.

Mitchell argues persuasively that this is a habit that does more harm than good. "People with marginal identities, as human beings, suffer all the frailties, inconsistencies, and failings of any other human," he writes. "We infantilize members of historically marginalized or oppressed groups by seeking to placate or pander instead of being in a right relationship, which requires struggle, debate, disagreement, and hard work. . . . Finding authentic alignment and solidarity among diverse voices is serious labor. After all, 'steel sharpens steel.'"

In other words, rather than allowing the necessary discomfort and challenge of substantive debate, identity essentialism wields identity as a blunt force weapon to coerce agreement and impose a twisted worldview where the value of ideas is entirely tied to the identity of the thinker—rather than the actual value or utility of the idea itself.

Within mainstream DEI work, identity essentialism manifests as dead-end debates over "who gets to speak." Workers pushing for trans rights come into friction with workers pushing to end sexual harassment, who in turn come into friction with workers pushing for racial justice, and all assert that their combination of identities makes their concerns the most legitimate and therefore worthy of taking priority over all others. The possibility that these issues could exist in tandem, connect deeply to each other, and be pursued collectively rarely gets recognized. Worse still, essentialism can warp into an inherently hostile stance against those without marginalized identities, regardless of their behaviors or perspectives. When straight, nondisabled White men are pushed to the side, excluded, or in rare cases, even demonized simply because of their lack of marginalized identities, progressive movements actively limit their own success and sow the seeds of future resentment and backlash.

Mitchell also calls attention to *maximalism*, or "considering anything less than the most idealistic position as a betrayal. . . . Relatedly, a righteous refusal to engage with people who do not already share our views and values." Within legacy DEI work, this tendency shows up most often in advocacy when the stakes feel high, serving as a motivating and rallying tactic for those most invested in creating change—which has the unfortunate side effect of putting off anyone with even slightly different views.

While engaging in student activism in my final year as an undergraduate in college, I experienced exactly this phenomenon when I was confronted by an activist peer in my dorm room, who was angry about an initiative I had undertaken in collaboration with university administrators to create change—administrators that this student was engaged in head-to-head conflict with.

"They're the enemy," my peer said, seething. "How could you do this to us? The only reason you should have reached out to them was so you could stab them in the back."

I still remember how I winced, my heartbeat loud in my ears and my palms sweaty. The implication of this peer's allegation was clear: I could not consider myself a "true activist" now that I had taken a stance that diverged from the most pure or dogmatic position, which he embodied, and I should be ashamed of my digression. It came as even more of a shock because I had previously considered this person a good acquaintance, if not a friend: we had supported each other several times after protest actions and saw each other perhaps every other week, on friendly terms. But the sudden hostility unnerved me. I couldn't help but feel that those feelings of intense threat and exclusion were exactly the point of the interaction: to enforce the shared beliefs and identity of the group, even if that meant sabotaging an initiative that would have furthered the group's goals.

To him, the confrontation to "bring me in line" likely was coming from a good place. He was scared that by diluting the message and people power of the movement, their efforts would fail and the status quo would stay harmful. It was ironic that the tactic he chose had virtually the same effect he was scared of: by refusing to expand the tent of the movement to everyone and refusing to build a coalition and movement made up of many different people, he was almost guaranteeing that his activism would fail to gain the critical mass it needed to actually succeed.

In a similar way within legacy DEI work, maximalism often emerges as a set of beliefs that prevents budding movements from building larger coalitions. Activist employees may scorn the ideas of engaging allies, reframing the goals of the movement in terms of win-win, or hearing the concerns of those not yet involved with the movement. Mitchell suggests that this shortcoming can be used "to justify not doing the basic work of organizing: talking to lots of different kinds of people on the doors, in their homes, and in their workplaces." "We need to meet people where they are, build relationships, and move them into action," he puts forward—a sentiment that many leading DEI practitioners also echo.

Finally, Mitchell covers the tendency toward *glass houses and small wars*, the tendency for those in movements to disproportionately insist that change (or worse, perfection) on the local or interpersonal scale be completely achieved before larger-scale change is initiated. I see this routinely in organizations, when well-intentioned DEI practitioners insist that leaders meet a high standard of interpersonal perfection as a litmus test for having their larger-scale decisions taken seriously. In its most self-defeating iteration, I once heard an employee suggest that their organization's pay equity audit be contested "because the leader who approved it still hasn't attended one of our ERG events and can't be trusted."

Trust is crucial, as I cover in a later chapter. But constantly seeking personal or interpersonal perfection over a more holistic view of change that pursues personal, interpersonal, organizational, and societal change in tandem can suck the oxygen out of the room—and ironically create organizations that are so obsessed with *saying* the right thing that they forget to actually utilize their influence to make a substantive difference. What can start as a well-intentioned desire to hold an organization to the same values it puts out into the world can, over time, twist into an exhausting negative spiral of self-directed criticism that can compromise its ability to function.

Mitchell is unflinchingly honest about the shortcomings of this "small utopianism" and highlights the need for both/and in this work. He emphasizes the need for greater tolerance of productive conflict without falling back on the constant comfort of purity and ideological agreement, slinging our siloed struggles at each other in a competition for attention and urgency, as the ERG leaders I worked with did. He isn't alone in calling for change. adrienne maree brown, writing on similar ideas, calls this "oppression Olympics on high alert: crisis Olympics. We do strange things as we compete with each other to bring attention to our work. We stop listening in a spirit of collaboration and start listening defensively, competitively, listening for where we are left out, or not at the top of the list; listening for where we must insert ourselves. As a result, we end up struggling to have conversations that can actually get us to the most strategic focus and action at any given moment."[2]

N'Tanya Lee discusses in that same article the alternative approach of *principled struggle*, "a way to struggle in which we are not being conflict avoidant, or conflict aggressive, but rather engaging in generative conflict, conflict that grows each of us and that creates more possibilities for what we can do in the world together. When we put our attention on conflict and difference in this way, it allows us to grow our capacity to be in integrity and unity with each other."

Workplace researchers back up these ideas with hard data. By successfully achieving an inclusive environment that replaces intergroup threat with safety for all, facilitates contact across difference, addresses inequality, and creates trust—you can build a workplace that simultaneously recognizes difference *and* feels cohesive and collaborative.[3] Conflict management research further elaborates: an inclusive environment allows for such a thing as "positive conflict"—conflict that preserves cohesion, increases satisfaction, and sources better ideas.[4]

If we are to call off the Oppression Olympics, we have to learn from these insights to push back against identity essentialism, maximalism, glass houses, and small wars with wiser tactics that actually work. In the workplace, that means no more binaries about "good" and "bad" people. No more talk of "oppressors" versus the "oppressed." No more single-issue struggles in siloed echo chambers, antagonistic rhetoric, and scorched earth tactics that sever relationships between communities and decision-makers.[5] In their stead, we need to do the hard work of strategizing and movement building *together*, bringing people into rooms that are designed to supply the respect, value, and safety needed to foster the messy, tough, yet productive conflict our workplaces and communities desperately need.

Building Winning Movements for All of Us

One of the enduring challenges within legacy DEI work has been navigating the twin extremes of movement building in the context of identity.

On the one hand, some leaders (and anti-DEI activists) argue that the only way to unify a workforce or community is to get rid of any mention of identity completely, to throw out the baby with the bathwater. Their stated desire is for a workplace that achieves gender parity without mentioning gender, racial equality without mentioning race, and so on. This is the premise behind their call for "colorblind" workplaces: that identity itself is divisive and enables discrimination. Research disagrees. When it comes to race, "colorblind" workplaces don't actually reduce racial discrimination; they just make it easier for White people to ignore it.[6] When identity-related talk is banned, identity-related discrimination is simply transformed into a format that is harder to track, without any change in harm or intensity. Want to make it socially unacceptable to talk about explicitly discriminating against mothers in hiring? If that's all you do, you'll simply convert that into discrimination against applicants with gaps in their employment history—a far more pernicious form of "legitimate" discrimination with a similarly devastating impact that continues to this day in the results of AI employment screens.[7]

On the other hand, leaders (and some DEI practitioners) argue that social identity is the end-all-be-all and allow their identity-centric DEI efforts to take over the culture of their entire workplaces. Their hope is that by making the language of identity the primary language of their organization (that is, framing every business decision and interpersonal interaction in the language of gender, race, sexuality, disability, and so on), they can draw attention to discrimination and create a better organization. Research disagrees. Beyond the harm that identity essentialism, maximalism, glass houses, and small wars can cause, the kind of shallow multiculturalism that results from this paradigm—where social groups are viewed through the lens of oversimplified cultural caricatures associated with stereotyped practices to "be inclusive"—can actually do more harm than good. This can lead to *worsened* stereotypes and increased resentment and backlash.[8] Interestingly enough, when I talk to ordinary people about DEI, they most frequently speak to these dysfunctions when they say that "DEI has gone too far."

What we need now is a third approach that learns from both of these ineffective strategies, an approach that recognizes the value of identity *and* the value of unity at the same time. We need an approach that follows the tenets of FAIR by achieving real results, changing systems and root causes, building strong coalitions, and communicating the win-win for all.

A powerful tool is the framework of *targeted universalism* developed by john a. powell, an American law professor and the Director of the UC Berkeley Othering and Belonging Institute.

Targeted universalism is a platform to operationalize programs that move all groups toward the universal policy goal as well as a way of communicating and publicly marketing such programs in an inclusive, bridging manner. It is an approach that supports the needs of particular groups, even the politically powerful or those in the majority, while reminding everyone that we are all part of the same social and civic fabric. As such, targeted universalist policies are more resistant to the critique that government programs serve special interests, whoever that might be.[9]

Targeted universalism starts by establishing a universal outcome that *all people* ought to experience. Say, respect. As an outcomes-centered and goal-oriented framework, targeted universalism makes it clear that until *everyone actually experiences respect*, the work must continue. How the work starts is with an impartial assessment of where there might be gaps or disparities in respect, with no preconceived notions about what that assessment might find.

For example, we can assess inclusion outcomes like respect (or value, or physical safety, or psychological safety) through survey questions directly asking about workers' perceptions across the organization. We can supplement these with valuable proxy metrics including the likelihood that employees recommend the organization as a place to work (also known as an employee Net Promoter Score, or eNPS) and HR metrics like retention rate, turnover intent, and absenteeism. By simultaneously collecting demographic data on dimensions of difference like race, gender, sexuality, age, ability, size, religion, nationality, and so on, we bring the necessary dimension of identity into our analysis—all while remaining agnostic about what findings emerge.

Almost every organization will find some room for improvement, but rarely are those opportunities evenly distributed across the organization. Whether due to biased environments, missing stairs, or other reasons, inequalities are likely to emerge that disadvantage some workers but not others. Targeted universalism guides us to name those groups explicitly and to be *targeted* in our approach to bring the standard for that group up to the *universal* goal that has been set, regardless of which group is having a worse experience. Under targeted universalism, if Black women experience the lowest rates of respect in the organization, then changemaking work should focus on improving the experience of Black women. Under targeted universalism, if straight White men experience the lowest rates of psychological safety in the organization, then changemaking work should focus on improving the experience of straight White men. The framework is identity conscious but simultaneously *value neutral*: there are no "good" or "bad" identities, no "oppressor" or "oppressed." There are simply people who have better or worse experiences of a universal outcome, who organizational leaders can design in partnership with to create real value, solve real problems, and build an organization that benefits more people.

Building movements with targeted universalism requires a fundamentally different way of thinking about this work compared to how it might take place within legacy DEI initiatives.

Legacy DEI sees movement building as gated behind identity and taking place in barely overlapping silos. An organization should have a dozen or more identity-related movements, including women leading efforts to fight sexism, disabled people leading efforts to fight ableism, LGBTQ+ people leading efforts to fight transphobia and homophobia, Latino people leading efforts to fight xenophobia and racism, and so on. Each of these movements, led by a clique of tight-knit advocates, seeks to achieve change by activating "allies," people who don't share an identity with those in the movement but hold some of the power and influence required to make change. Just as Asian American employees might seek allies among their White, Latino, Black, and Indigenous colleagues, Black employees might seek allies among their White, Latino, Asian American, and Indigenous colleagues, and so on.

Imagine you're a well-intentioned employee who has the time to attend events from every ERG in your organization and receive every call to action presented in these events. From the women's ERG, you'd receive five practices for fighting sexism. From the disability ERG and LGBTQ+ ERG, you'd receive five practices each for fighting ableism and anti-LGBTQ+ discrimination, respectively. From each of your four race-related ERGs, you'd receive five practices for fighting anti-Black, anti-Asian, anti-Latino, and anti-Indigenous bias, respectively. You'd take back to your desk the earnest yet impossible commitment to apply thirty-five different practices every day, in order to be a good ally to each of these movements. (And if your organization has religion-, age-, or parent-focused ERGs as well, then you do the math.)

What happens more often than not is that individuals, overwhelmed with the burden of individual allyship, choose to do nothing instead— and in response to that inaction, each social movement steps up its tactics to frame its issues as ever more urgent and ever more dire, in a constant competition over limited time and attention that burns out everyone involved with no change to show for it.

This was the doom spiral that the Fortune 500 company's ERGs found themselves in when I entered their organization. To end it, my colleagues and I had to interrupt the cycle and reframe the work of movement building around the goal of benefits for *everyone*, not just "more for me." Targeted universalism, the curb-cut effect, and change management all came in handy here.

We started by asking every group, every employee, and every executive exactly what mattered most to them and what outcome was most lacking that needed to be present. We asked ERG members and non-ERG members alike. We asked DEI advocates and anti-DEI advocates alike. The most common answer was surprisingly simple: people over and over again told us, "We just want to feel valued." Alongside that answer, we learned something incredible. Black workers believed that they were the only ones in the organization who were undervalued. Straight White men *also* believed that they were the only ones in the organization who felt undervalued. Practically every group saw itself as the "most marginalized"—and yet, the data we collected showed that nearly every group outside of executives felt similarly undervalued, and their complaints were nearly identical.

It was this experience of scarcity and threat that pushed everyone into zero-sum rhetoric and competition with one another, when focusing instead on *abundance* might have helped them realize that they had much in common with each other. So that's what we did. We matter-of-factly shared the results of the survey, alongside a simple call to action: the question "In our work to make this workplace better value everyone in it, how can we make sure it better values *people like you?*"

And with those constructive recommendations as a starting point, we brought people together and started a conversation about what a more inclusive organization would look like—for everyone.

Now, as proud as I am of this work, I won't sugarcoat it: it wasn't smooth sailing after this point. It was movement building in all its messy glory. Maurice Mitchell inspirationally speaks to "steel sharpening steel," but if I'm honest, it was really more like trying to cook a Michelin-star-worthy meal with no plan and a hundred anxious chefs in the kitchen, each with something to prove.

It was an uphill battle the entire way, and without having built a strong foundation for productive conflict, people were eager to avoid the discomfort. I received constant requests from nervous leaders to "give people more things to do," or "suggest practices that everyone can start using immediately." (I resisted—I've learned my lesson since my very first DEI-related role, when I made that list of "do's and don'ts" against my better judgment.)

What people want to hear is that no matter what inclusion issue exists in their organization, any employee who attends an optional DEI-related event can always make a difference with one or two easy, frictionless practices that they can learn in sixty minutes or less. But this tendency to chase the dopamine hit of "doing something over nothing," or the low-hanging fruit of "easy, visible action *now*," over the challenging work of long-term change is exactly how internal movements get warped into the identity essentialism, maximalism, glass houses, and small wars that Mitchell writes about, as they pursue actions that craft the appearance of change over the messiness of actually effecting it.

I once told a group of internal DEI champions that "heroes get magic; movements need supply chains."

The saying is meant to challenge the idea that we can create change simply by imagining ourselves as individual heroes who, through our own passion or expertise, can change harmful systems on our own or by compelling those in power to do what we say. As appealing as this belief may sound, it doesn't line up with the reality of making change. If there's anything that a passionate individual can do to make change, it's to let go of their ego and channel their energy into creating a robust, well-resourced, and committed coalition that channels people power at scale. Sexy? Ego validating? Perhaps not. But that's what it takes to make real change.

Collective action is everything, and there's a formula for getting it right. To set a movement up for success, you have to create reciprocal relationships of mutual benefit, foster trust between different segments of your organization or social groups involved in that movement, and establish collaboration norms that allow different groups to share the load of challenging tasks. Researchers call this state *organizational solidarity*, and they're clear that there are no shortcuts to getting there: solidarity must be earned over time rather than ordered into being.[10] How? Bring people together as often as you can make it happen. Invest in connection across differences as much as, or even more than, connection among those with shared identities. With constant contact, bounded by good facilitation and strong norms, you'll build strong relationships. With strong relationships, you'll build trust and safety. With trust and safety, you'll enable productive conflict no matter how explosive or dynamic that conflict might feel in the moment.

Organizational solidarity, successfully built over time, transcends the transactional and zero-sum nature that many well-intentioned inclusion efforts get trapped in, and turns potentially toxic and zero-sum conflict into something more productive. Rather than groups engaging in conflict over whose problems are *most important*, organizational solidarity allows groups to engage in conflict over *how to best fight their shared problems* and, in doing so, expand the pie for everyone. The research agrees. Simply reframing the issues we work on away from pointing fingers at "problematic groups" and toward bringing groups together to focus on "shared problems" can dramatically improve engagement from skeptics and mitigate backlash—to everyone's benefit.[11] By engaging everyone in part of the solution, you can pursue initiatives that *work* for the good of all.[12]

6

REPRESENTATION IS LEADERSHIP YOU TRUST

> REPRESENTATION is when all people trust those who lead them to understand and operate with their needs and interests in mind, regardless of those leaders' social identities.

I once worked with a women-led and majority-women organization that was dealing with a peculiar problem: a persistent accusation from entry- to mid-level employees that the organization didn't represent women. The leadership of the organization was exasperated. "We're obviously all women. How much more 'representative of women' could we get? These folks need to listen to women—to listen to *us*."

Frustrated employees had little patience for this deflection. "Just because our leaders are women doesn't mean they speak for us. Just look at their recent return-to-office mandate. If they actually know the benefits that flexible work has for women, they're not acting like it. Our leaders need to listen to women—to listen to *us*."

Both leadership and employee critics were partially correct, but each was missing something essential. Leadership was correct that their team *was* entirely made up of women. But they were also mistakenly assuming that, simply because they checked the identity box of being women, they not only understood the needs of all women in the organization but were also entitled to support from them. Employee critics were correct that their all-women leadership team was broadly out of touch with the needs of women elsewhere in their organization. But they were also mistaken in arguing that simply because their executives were women, they ought to know about, agree with, and push forward specific policies that were perceived as being "good for women."

In the previous chapter, we explored some of the most common traps that well-intentioned social movements and organizations can fall into: purity politics, identity essentialism, maximalism, glass houses, and small wars. In this majority-women workplace, both leadership and employee critics were engaging in identity essentialism, leveling competing assertions at each other that leaders' identities as women either necessitated support from other women or necessitated support for specific policies perceived to favor women. But as we have learned, essentialism makes for dead-end debates and is a poor replacement for substantive conversation.

To fix this workplace's issues, they had to tackle challenges that ran far deeper than the gender box leaders or employees checked, challenges linked to trust, communication, and leadership that had long been masked by DEI-related language from both groups. A fix would not come just from replacing their leadership with "better women" like some employees wanted. Nor would it come from teaching their employees to "better respect women" like some leaders wanted. The only path forward was to rebuild trust the hard way, by collectively working through the answers to tough questions about identity and leadership. What did it mean to promote themselves as "women led?" What commitments to women were actually part of the organization's values or purpose, and how did those manifest? What were the needs of employees in the organization? What were the expectations placed on leadership, especially those related to identity, and the costs of violating those expectations?

It may appear that few of these issues relate directly to representation, at least not in the way that legacy DEI efforts tend to frame it. But within the FAIR Framework, representation looks a little different than it does under legacy DEI. Rather than being a numbers game to be won when enough people have checked the desired demographic boxes, representation as described in FAIR is a measure of the *trust* that different organizational groups place in a given leadership team, organization, product, or outcome.

Under this model, for a group—say, women—to achieve representation in leadership, that group must *trust leadership to represent their perspectives and needs*, regardless of the identities of individual leaders.

Using this new definition of representation, we can make sense of the paradoxical story with which I opened this chapter. Most employees in the organization did not feel represented by their leadership team, despite sharing the same identity as "women," because they didn't *trust* that team to represent their perspectives and needs. Until leaders successfully rebuilt that trust by taking into account their employees' perspectives and needs, representation would still be lacking.

The new definition certainly helps bring a new perspective to this particular story. But why the reframing in the first place? Because I can think of few other aspects of legacy DEI efforts that have resulted in so many cobra effects and unintended consequences as "representation measured by boxes checked." A sober look back through the last thirty years of workplace DEI impact shows that the public's single-minded focus on representational gains as the most obvious marker of "DEI progress" was exploited. Rather than achieving greater representation through better pipelines, fairer processes, more inclusive cultures, and more collaborative decisions, employers created their own parallel industry to give the illusion of representative gains without any real change.

As entire industries have sprung up to help "increase representation," the actual percentages of people from underrepresented backgrounds in positions of leadership have scarcely budged.

In 1985, Black men made up 3 percent of management teams within US companies with 100 or more employees. In 2016, that number had moved "up" to a whopping 3.2 percent.[1] While nearly 29 percent of American adults have a disability, only 7 percent of corporate boards have even a single board member with a disability.[2] Despite collectively making up 42 percent of the overall American population, people of color make up 26 percent of the 119th US Congress.[3] Despite making up 50.5 percent of the US population, women make up only 10.7 percent of leadership positions within Fortune 500 companies.[4]

Despite the stagnation of real representational gains, employers have only become more savvy at showing the public what they know the public wants to see. By installing and valorizing a small number of under-represented faces in high places, or *tokens*, employers effectively give the appearance of representational gains while also propping up these tokens as a shield against criticism. The underlying inequalities and harmful environments that prevent other people from an underrepresented population from ascending into leadership go entirely unchanged, while a superficial number of "opportunities" cycle among the small pool of leaders allowed to ascend. For example, in a high-profile story from 2020, a seventy-six-year-old Black board director shared how over the course of his career, he held *fourteen board of director roles*—and companies continued to offer him more positions even after he retired rather than finding new candidates.[5]

This trend, undertaken by leadership teams to protect themselves from the ire of their progressive employees, customers, and investors, fundamentally undermines their own stated values of fairness and merit by institutionalizing the notion that the current dominance of straight, White, male leadership can only be maintained through deceit. If right-wing extremism aims to sow the false narrative that there is no future for straight White men under a DEI-friendly future save that of inevitable irrelevance and disempowerment, the cynical decisions of corporate leadership have essentially told those very men with a wink and a nudge, "Maybe, but we'll drag our feet as long as we can." It's insulting, to say the least.

We can do far better than that, not just for underrepresented groups or those invested in DEI, but for straight White men as well. By reframing representation as a matter of trust, not identitarian box-checking, we can break the cynical paradigm wide open and build a future where *everyone feels represented and no one feels replaced*, a future where we can build benefit for all without the shadow of zero-sum looming over us.

Under the FAIR Framework, trust is both the goal and the pathway to achieving representation. When any group feels underrepresented, it's because *they don't trust* the thing they're engaging with, whether it be a leadership team, a piece of media, or an organizational policy. Creating that sense of representation requires deeper and more substantive solutions than changing the boxes that individual people check—it requires rebuilding trust by meeting the needs of an audience, creating value, demonstrating transparency, and problem-solving together.

Legacy DEI might look at a team of ten people and ask, "How many of those ten people are women? Are people of color? Have a disability? Are LGBTQ+?" Based on the static answer, legacy DEI would issue an either/or verdict: "diverse" or "not diverse." The only path forward to progress under this model is necessarily zero-sum: if the group isn't "diverse enough," then men, White people, nondisabled people, and straight people better make way for their replacements. No matter how much we might try to justify it, you're still telling someone at the end of the day that you're coming for their job—and if they have any power to leverage, you can be sure that they'll try to stop you with it.

FAIR might look at the same team and ask, "To what extent is this team *trusted* by women? People of color? People with disabilities? LGBTQ+ people? How about men, White people, nondisabled people, or straight people? What needs of these groups has the team met? What value has it created? How transparently has it done so? How well has it brought these groups into its decision-making process?" These questions lead to far more interesting and actionable answers than those asked by legacy DEI. The path forward they promise is one that centers action and results, rather than box-checking. It seeks to solve problems by addressing the root causes of mistrust rather than giving the same harmful structures a friendly face. It offers a role for any leader, regardless of identity, in the work of repairing and building trust—rather than blaming or tokenizing them for the identities they hold. And most of all, it articulates a vision of the future that turns the threat of zero-sum "replacement" on its head, focusing unflinchingly on the potential for a better and more trusting world for all of us.

How do we get there? We start by understanding how we got into our mess of tokenization, so we can get ourselves out of it.

We Deserve More Than Tokens

Activists, advocates, and communities of people who have historically been underrepresented in society have always fought for a world where they are valued just as much as their peers, a world that sees, validates, and empowers their full humanity as it does for others.

Representational parity, an outcome where leaders of workplaces and societies proportionally resemble the people they lead, was envisioned as the ultimate indicator of progress, a way to visualize the endpoint of a society or workplace that has successfully removed its barriers and achieved fairness, access, inclusion, and representation for everyone. As a result of fair recruitment, hiring, development, evaluation, promotion, and leadership practices, there's little reason why the identities of leaders wouldn't statistically reflect the identities of the populations they serve, after all. If 29 percent of adults have a disability, shouldn't 29 percent of leaders and board members have a disability, too? If 50 percent of the population are women, then shouldn't 50 percent of executives be women, too?

The concept of representational parity let us frame our aspirations with clarity and specificity—but as it turned out, it didn't help us actually achieve them.

In today's world, organizations that successfully go from entirely homogeneous to having some small amount of demographic diversity, whether by gender, race, disability, age, sexuality, or otherwise, tend to stop after making that first bit of progress. Many of us have seen it firsthand.

An all-male, all-White board of directors will take great pains to hire one woman and one non-White person and then, seemingly satisfied, will drop all efforts to diversify and will maintain that status quo however it can. For example, research finds that corporate boards tend to replace departing board members with successors possessing the exact same demographic characteristics—ensuring that White people are replaced with other White people, Black people are replaced with other Black people, and so on.[6] This strategy actively prevents the racial makeup of the board from changing, with everyone locked into their roles. Those who aren't White, straight, or male get the memo pretty quickly: their presence is superficial, and they shouldn't expect that to change.

Tokenism describes the cynical practice of elevating one or a small number of people to (often symbolic) positions of power as a ploy to deflect criticism. Far from being an isolated practice of leadership abuse, tokenism is one of the primary tools that homogeneous industries and environments have used for decades to survive in increasingly pluralistic societies without needing to fundamentally change who they are or what they do. Civil rights leader Martin Luther King Jr. spoke precisely about this phenomenon in 1960:

> Many areas in the South are retreating to a position where they will permit a handful of Negroes to attend all-white schools or allow the employment in lily-white factories of one Negro to a

thousand whites. Thus, we have advanced in some places from all-out, unrestrained resistance to a sophisticated form of delaying tactics, embodied in tokenism.[7]

Documented across the creative industry, the restaurant industry, publishing, business, and other sectors, tokenism is a deeply entrenched strategy with a seductive logic. Both the institutions using it *and* those selected as the honorary token benefit, at the cost of heavily restricting all others in the token's social group from social advancement. For the token, it's a Faustian bargain.

Tokens experience greater stress, isolation, scrutiny, and pressure to perform, and receive less support from their colleagues.[8] In particular, tokens face heavy pressure to *not* look as though they act in preferential ways toward their ingroup members, for fear of being punished by peers in their new environment.[9] This pressure often forces token leaders to choose between their own success at the price of upholding the status quo power structures, or advocating for marginalized communities, knowing that this will compromise their standing, if not their careers, as leaders.

In the grand scheme of things, tokenism maintains inequality. Psychologists have found that when men and women are exposed to tokenistic practices—for example, learning that a group predominantly made up of men has one woman in it—they come away with different but complementary conclusions that both maintain the status quo.[10] Men in this experiment who might have expressed concerns about fairness in response to an all-male group felt those concerns entirely alleviated when exposed to tokenism, as if they thought, "If there is one woman, then we cannot be sexist." Women in this experiment who might have rightly assumed that they had no chance for advancement in response to the all-male group instead held onto hope that advancement was possible when exposed to tokenism, as if they thought, "If there is one woman, then maybe there's a chance for me to get there too." Rather than increasing people's enthusiasm for positive change, tokenism more often prolongs our tolerance and acceptance of the unequal status quo.

We deserve better than tokens, but we often lack the imagination to know what "better" looks like. We hold onto a single vision for the arc of change: a lone trailblazer earns their spot among a previously homogeneous group and establishes themself as the "first." That first leader of their kind beats the odds and lifts up another, and then another, and another, until finally the homogeneous group looks a little more like the world they serve. Whether they ask for it or not, we impose that desperate narrative onto every trailblazer we find, in the hopes that they can single-handedly change their entire environment for the better—and when they fail, we criticize them and their organization for letting us down.

Underlying this pattern is our core dependence on identity essentialism: the belief that no one can make us feel heard, valued, inspired, or led except for those who check the same identity boxes.

This was the fallacy made by the women-led, majority-women organization: that identity was a proxy for leadership. This is the source of the extreme pressure tokens face to succeed as visible representations of their entire social groups. This is the driver of our bottomless frustration when we see leaders who look like us replicating the same harms of the status quo they inherit.

But throughout this entire process, in putting these impossibly high expectations on members of marginalized groups, *we don't question for a second when we put equally low expectations on the existing leaders of the status quo.*

We look at male leaders and think that in no world could they ever be people who might represent women. We dismiss on sight the possibility that they might ever understand women's needs to such an extent that they could use their power to remove barriers, eliminate discrimination, and create resources to support and empower women.

We look at White leaders and think that in no world could they ever be people who might represent Black, Latino, Indigenous, Asian, or mixed-race people. We dismiss on sight the possibility that they might ever be seen as champions for racialized people, and assume that the best they could ever do is to "get out of our way."

We assume the best that people with power and privilege can do is to "pass the mic." To "shut up and learn." We interpret the rallying cry of "nothing about us without us"—to me, a powerful call for embedding the perspectives of the groups we design for into every decision-making process we use—as "If you're not us, your role is to do nothing." And yet despite all this, we stare in shock when we hear the statistic that nearly 70 percent of White men are unsure if DEI work is supposed to include them.[11]

We will never break out of our paradigm of tokenism until we stop expecting that tokenized minorities can single-handedly end inequality, and start expecting more from majority leaders, who in many of our organizations are White men. (In other countries and contexts, you may just as readily substitute members of the dominant or most powerful social groups, who are typically overrepresented in leadership.) If we want to be FAIR, we have to see our leaders—regardless of their identities—as being more than capable of building trust with every community that looks to them to lead.

So they might be all men, or all White, or all straight, or nondisabled, or rich, or Christian. We can shift systems to create a more representative future while holding the present leadership to the same standards as everyone they claim to lead. Their collective lack of demographic representativeness isn't a free pass to be ignorant. It's simply a different starting point for them to become leaders that people can trust.

Same goes if they're all women, or all Asian, Latino, Black, Indigenous, or mixed race, or disabled, or Muslim, or Jewish, or queer, or trans. Their presence does not guarantee that the systems they steward are the best they can be. And by no means do they get a free pass to do harm just because they might check the right boxes. Their identities simply give them a different starting point to become leaders that people can trust.

Earning Trust, One Win at a Time

I want you to imagine a leadership team for me: a small one, composed of just three people. To make these hypothetical leaders feel more real, let's distribute some identities—one is a nondisabled, straight, nonreligious White man in his forties; the second is a straight, Christian White man with a disability in his fifties; and the third is a nondisabled, straight Latina woman in her thirties.

If you sell to US-based customers, is the team representative of your customer base?

If we go through the usual talking points, we can find ourselves quickly coming up against some awkward obstacles.

Women make up 50.5 percent of the American population. So should there be one woman, or two? America's racial demographics are around 60 percent (non-Hispanic) White, 18.5 percent Hispanic, 12.2 percent Black, 5.6 percent Asian, 2.8 percent mixed race or multiracial, and 0.9 percent Native American, Hawaiian, or Pacific Islander. So who should the third leadership seat go to? Should the first two even go to White people in the first place?

Don't forget that 13 percent of the population has a disability and that 9.3 percent of American adults identify as part of the LGBTQ+ community. You can't miss, either, that 13 percent of the American workforce is between 16 and 24, 22 percent is between 25 and 34, 22 percent is between 35 and 44, 20 percent is between 45 and 54, and 23 percent is older than 54. So who should be what identity for this team to be truly representative?

In my experience, follow this line of reasoning for any longer than a brief moment and most people will readily admit its uselessness. Even if you could optimally distribute identities into a "perfect" distribution of representativeness and then find qualified people who meet those criteria, it would be nearly impossible to become perfectly representative in this way without setting ourselves up as some omnipotent arbiter of diversity enforcement. But even then, when people look to leadership teams, they still find themselves thinking things like, "I want to see myself reflected in this team. I want to feel heard. I want to be inspired." We find ourselves wishing nonetheless that one person on the team shares an identity with us—even if statistically unlikely—because we hope that by dint of that shared identity, they might understand us.

Identity essentialism is deeply validating, yet it limits us all the same. A transgender colleague once bemoaned in the middle of a conversation that "we wouldn't be seeing so many antitransgender policies if we had more transgender people in government." A South Asian friend once told me that, now that another South Asian professional had been promoted to manager for the first time in his company, the belittling attitude of the management team would soon change. "Representation changes everything," he insisted. Struggling to imagine feeling valued, heard, or inspired unless we see someone with a relatable face and story, we desperately look for tokens and ignore the deeper manifestations of our values that have more to do with behavior and little to do with identity alone: fairness, transparency, benefit, inclusion, and so much more.

But at this point, we have powerful tools at our disposal to do better. In particular, we've explored numerous strategies for moving beyond our frozen status quo, defusing backlash, and rebuilding trust beyond the confines of legacy DEI—staying focused the entire time on achieving results, solving root causes beyond individuals, building broad coalitions, and communicating the win-win.

When people trust those who lead them to represent their perspectives and needs, that's representation—regardless of those leaders' individual identities. And to build that trust, the first step is to help people feel that their needs are heard. Remember inclusive and universal design processes? Both require that decision-makers shift from their default top-down decision-making process to instead make decisions in partnership with the communities they lead. While that doesn't mean leaders will *always* do what their audiences want, more participatory decision-making processes like these can give people a voice and help them feel that their insight matters, no matter where in the organization they sit.[12]

The process itself is just the start; what we share about it can allow us to go further. Transparency, achieved by sharing enough internal communication for people to understand how and why decisions are made, builds trust and improves the reputation of leadership.[13] To build transparency, you can start by talking about how the decision-making processes in your organization work.

How are senior leaders *actually* hired? How are powerful clients and external partnerships *actually* chosen? How are promotions *actually* decided, projects *actually* taken, and conflicts *actually* resolved? Rather than taking the defensive posture of restricting information and preparing to justify the status quo, allow yourself the vulnerability of being honest and accepting the possibility that the status quo will change in response to feedback. If the actual method of bringing on senior leaders is "Jeff reaches out to his past colleagues from other organizations," then you're likely to get some pushback, and rightly so. The way you deal with that pushback will determine whether you build trust or lose it. If you want people to accept and trust the leaders you hire, whether or not each leader checks a certain identity box, you need them to trust the process by which you bring those leaders in. (Your "Jeff network" doesn't make the cut, to be clear.)

Don't forget the principle we covered all the way back in chapter 1: we build trust when we deliver real value for the people we serve. Somehow, even after all we've explored, it still sounds like a radical idea when said out loud.

Leaders: if your sales team is complaining that their work is made harder by a new hire onboarding process that lasts only two days, you build trust with sales by solving that problem. Not by holding an event celebrating the importance of sales. Not by bringing in an external sales influencer to discuss how to onboard in two days. Not by blustering that, because you yourself have a background in sales, those salespeople owe you their loyalty by dint of shared identity. You build trust by solving the problem, period. Your solution will have a cost, yes—but that cost will be far lower than the cost of letting the problem fester, and the gains in trust are priceless.

Building trust within FAIR work is no different. If women in your organization are complaining that a lack of flexible work is damaging their well-being, you build trust with women by solving that problem, period. You may not end up developing the same solution as the one they suggest at first, and that's OK. So long as you make a good-faith effort to work together, solve your people's problems and address their needs, do so earnestly and respectfully, and achieve real results, you'll see returns in the form of trust.

This is the advice I gave to the women-led organization whose story I shared at the beginning of the chapter. I advised their leadership team to let go of their egos, work to truly understand their employees' needs, and deliver real wins in whatever form that took. And with wins in hand, they could gain the trust to ask harder questions, get harder answers, deliver even bigger wins, and gain even more trust. If they could stay on that path, they could become more than simply a women-led organization—they could become an organization that women trusted.

A final note that trust is a constantly fluctuating give-and-take, not a one-time journey. I once worked with an organization that regularly surveyed their workforce and secured about an 80 percent response rate with every survey. But after one such survey, their HR leader made a careless statement during an all-hands meeting that indicated that these surveys were a low priority and the data was rarely leveraged to inform any changemaking efforts. Employees took note: the next survey received only a dismal 40 percent response rate.

"What strategies can we use to get our response rate back up to 80 percent?" the HR leader asked me during one of our sessions. I shook my head.

"Forty percent is the number of people that trust you to make change right now," I responded. "It was 80, but right now it's 40. The most sustainable way you can bring that number back up is to regain their lost trust, by demonstrating that you take these surveys seriously."

The HR department took these words to heart. Following that survey, they engaged in an in-depth campaign to act on employees' recommendations to build a more inclusive workplace, during which they communicated heavily about the usefulness of survey feedback. I received word from the HR leader later that year that their subsequent survey's response rate had recovered to 65 percent. It was a good start. With any luck, and continued consistency in follow-through, trust would only continue to recover.

The legacy DEI paradigm of checkbox representation asks, "Do we have enough women?" "Do we have enough Black people, or Asian people, or Latino people?" It asks of marketing and promotion materials, "Do we depict enough disabled people?" "Do we show enough religious minorities?" "Is there an LGBTQ+ person?"

But representation built on trust requires more substantial tests that go beyond head-counting and box-checking. It asks, "Are women being treated fairly here?" "Do Black people, Asian people, and Latino people feel like their needs are being met?" "Are we the best place to work for people with disabilities?" "Are religious minorities safe here?" "Do LGBTQ+ people feel like their voices matter here?"

And these questions are far from reserved only for members of marginalized groups. You might find equally valuable insights from asking yourself these same questions about men, straight people, White people, and so on. Remember that when it comes to achieving FAIR outcomes in organizations rich in difference, we must be willing to embrace any and all differences—so long as we learn from them to come together and build better environments for us all. Any leader, any product team, any team, and any person can answer these questions regardless of their identities. Being representative in this way means having done the work to build trust and to walk the talk with each and every one of the many social and organizational groups that make up our pluralistic workplaces, demographic box-checking be damned.

There's just one last question to answer: What of numerical representation? At the start of this chapter, I lamented the stagnation of our societal progress on achieving representational gains and harshly criticized the prevalence of tokenism as a distraction from real progress. Trust, I argued, was a more actionable outcome to base our understanding of representation on.

Does that mean we should give up on seeing representational parity in leadership? Give up on the hope that one day, our leaders not only speak to our needs, but look like us, too?

Not in the slightest. We can and should continue to strive for representational parity at every level, from the makeup of candidates hired to the executives promoted and the board members selected—but as a lagging indicator of fairness by design, not as a metric to impose by fiat.

How? By creating broadly representative candidate pools; using structured interviewing and hiring panels; implementing salary transparency; recruiting more effectively from a broad range of sources; creating lasting relationships of mutual benefit with professional organizations, institutions of higher learning, customers, and local communities; training hiring managers to use bias interrupters; tracking aggregated demographics throughout the hiring process; and adopting other practices that make the hiring process more fair for all. Implementing each of these practices will take organizational change to identify unfairness and correct the disparities. Building buy-in will require a well-crafted narrative that leans on the curb-cut effect. Sustaining progress without backlash is more likely with targeted universalism as a strategy for intervention.

Representational parity is possible, but the work of removing systemic barriers that restrict people's potential, eliminate discrimination, and set everyone up for success will take time. In parallel, the leaders we've got today must put in the work to become leaders that everyone can trust.

7

THE FUTURE OF FAIRNESS

I write this book amid one of the most threatening backslides of democratic norms that the United States has ever experienced. As authoritarianism surges, anxieties swell, and inequality worsens, the ideal of a brighter future offering greater opportunity for all seems all but subsumed by our feelings of fear and threat.

And yet, central to this book is the idea that better is possible. That building a world—or at the very least, an organization—that pushes back inequality, expands opportunity, and safeguards fairness is possible. While Americans may disagree (oftentimes, bitterly) about how and why this needs to happen, they *do* largely agree that it needs to happen. Sociologist and political scientist Leslie McCall, in researching Americans' perspectives on inequality, finds that a comfortable majority want the status quo to change and for major institutions to drive it. "If you combine the share of people who say the government is responsible or that private companies are responsible, it's about two-thirds of Americans. Two-thirds of people want a major institution—the government or private companies—to reduce inequality."[1]

That people ought to have a fair shot at achieving success, regardless of who they are or what background they come from is a fundamentally American ideal. People may often disagree over whether this American

Dream still exists today, but a stunning supermajority—94 percent, according to the Pew Research Center—believe that it at least existed at some time.[2] Reviving social progress, restoring the possibility of upward mobility, and expanding the opportunity for all people to have the social and economic thriving and dignity they deserve remains an absolutely essential project.

Organizations are microcosms of society: the same issues we deal with on a national scale are often present closer to home. And while the prospect of making change on a societal scale might feel daunting, those of us who work, volunteer, or otherwise participate in organizations can far more manageably envision changing our workplaces, community organizations, or even our informal friend groups for the better.

This is precisely why I developed FAIR and the FAIR Framework: to give more of us the tools we need to make a difference, not just with our good intentions alone, but with the kinds of evidence-based practices we need to succeed in these tense, polarized times.

I'm far from the only person working on these issues. But from my perspective, experience, and research, I'm seeing far too many well-intentioned leaders and practitioners respond to this moment with solutions that won't solve our problems. It feels like being on a conveyor belt moving slowly toward a meat grinder, and thinking that walking in the opposite direction will save us. Our only choice is to think and do differently than we've done before—to do the equivalent of hopping off the conveyor belt and hitting the stop button, even if it feels like "breaking the rules" to do so.

What are those rules?

That good intentions matter most. That self-help is all we need. That duct tape fixes broken systems. That the Oppression Olympics is worth competing in. That shared identity matters more than tangible progress.

Some of these rules originate from our environments as reactionary efforts to resist change or evolution. Some originate from our own personal and community histories of trauma or scarcity. Some originate from our strong moral beliefs about the importance of change and social progress. But whether we intend for it or not, these spoken and unspoken rules have compromised the vision and execution of our efforts to build better organizations. Until we cast them off, and find the courage to lead differently from before, we'll find ourselves treading water without making progress.

As an industry and as a people, we have been here before. The work that was until recently called diversity, equity, and inclusion was once called diversity and inclusion, which was once called diversity management, which was once called affirmative action. What some don't realize is that the events that gave "DEI" its starting point as "diversity" work almost perfectly mirror our present day.

In the years following the civil rights movement, as affirmative action was achieving striking wins in increasing the representation of Black Americans in higher education and in workplaces across the country, backlash to progress simmered. During the Reagan administration, the rhetoric of "reverse racism" was emboldened and cultivated until the idea that affirmative action policies were themselves racist took hold. As the Reagan administration dismantled civil rights protections, legal challenges against affirmative action mounted until finally the Supreme Court outlawed race-conscious admissions in colleges. Affirmative action became the scapegoat and punching bag of Reagan's campaign; his administration used the Justice Department to attack affirmative action programs, and his lieutenants undermined civil rights laws and their enforcement.[3] Those doing affirmative action work were all but forced to adopt the watered-down language of "diversity" put forth by the Supreme Court in its 1978 *Regents of the University of California v. Bakke* decision and change their tactics accordingly—the zeitgeist had so thoroughly turned against affirmative action that the phrase itself was tarnished and remains so in the US to this day.

In the mid-2020s, we find ourselves experiencing an eerily reminiscent pendulum swing, not just away from social progress but aggressively toward fascism and authoritarianism. Anti-DEI attacks are just one of the many avenues through which right-wing extremists are targeting well-established American institutions, seeking a pretense to dismantle, defang, or destroy potential opposition, whether nonprofits, institutions of higher learning, or private corporations.[4]

Keeping our heads down will not save us. Nor will staying the course with our ineffective efforts to create change, which are unlikely to become more effective over time but increasingly mark us as targets for retaliation and persecution, even if we try to shift our language.

Rebranding DEI as "FAIR" will not save us. But *reimagining* how we conceptualize and execute what we used to call DEI just might, and the FAIR Framework was created explicitly to evolve legacy DEI into a far more defensible platform than exists at present.

In the introduction of this book, I shared the damning statistic that only 20 percent of workers felt like DEI had directly benefited them. In part, these low numbers almost certainly emerge from a communications deficit: if DEI leaders and practitioners communicated as often about the value of the Americans with Disabilities Act, parental leave benefits, workers' rights, and other wins achieved through progressive social movements as they do about cultural heritage celebrations, perhaps worker sentiment would be very different. But we have to reckon with the possibility that people don't believe DEI has benefited them because that's just true: it hasn't.

Their workplace held a cultural heritage celebration, but they were still overlooked for a promotion in favor of the less-qualified employee they helped train. Their workplace paid for an expensive inclusion award, but their coworkers still mock them for their accent. They attended a training on allyship, but their manager never showed up. They fill out surveys, volunteer for interviews, and maybe even organize an event or two, but their working experience never changes for the better.

This possibility should be unacceptable for every leader and practitioner committed to DEI, and yet many have resigned themselves to ineffectiveness. "We don't have the funding for impact." "We can't help but preach to the choir when the bad apples choose not to attend." "We're making baby steps, and that counts for something." "Something is better than nothing."

Throughout this book, I've sought to make the case that "something" is *not* always better than nothing.

I've shared how cobra effects, the unintended consequences of our good intentions, can worsen the very problems we aim to solve. How in taking the path of least resistance or pursuing the lowest-hanging fruit, the very people working to make positive change can inadvertently tip the scales in the opposite direction.

I've shared how the most popular and common tools of legacy DEI may leave our workplaces expecting change that never comes and sow the seeds of future backlash. I told the story of how the tension between what organizations and leaders are willing to invest in and what practices actually work puts practitioners in the compromising position of balancing our values, our livelihoods, and our desired impact—with impact most often being what we choose to sacrifice, to the detriment of legacy DEI's effectiveness.

I've dissected the most common failures of legacy DEI and pulled out four fatal mistakes that programs make:

1. **Getting caught up in our good intentions and ignoring the real outcomes we seek to achieve.** Do we choose to measure and celebrate how many people attend our events, or what changes as the result of it? Do we reward people for committing to change, or for achieving it?

2. **Ignoring systemic causes in favor of self-help.** Are we changing behavior by gambling on self-help at scale, or are we changing the organization and bringing everyone along?

3. **Choosing to remain in narrow cliques at the expense of powerful coalitions.** Do we expand the tent to create collective change, or worship our own purity as people who "get it"?

4. **Using zero-sum rhetoric to antagonize at the cost of building movements using the win-win.** Are we building a better world together, or sowing the seeds of future resentment for short-term gratification?

From these, I've reconstructed four tenets that set apart FAIR from legacy DEI:

1. **FAIR looks beyond good intentions to center efforts that achieve results.**

2. **FAIR looks beyond self-help to solve for the root cause of our problems.**

3. **FAIR looks beyond narrow cliques to build broad coalitions across difference.**

4. **FAIR looks beyond the ease of zero-sum rhetoric to always find the win-win.**

The term "FAIR" is catchy, simple, and easy to define. I like it, but it's by no means the only option for those looking to evolve their DEI work. I know of several other proposed evolutions of DEI work, from a focus on Belonging, to a simplification back to Inclusion, to a reformatting as simply Leadership. Call your work FAIR or not; so long as you *do* the work more effectively, I consider us all working toward the same goals.

But the four tenets are nonnegotiable.

Whatever we call the work, we must center real outcomes and real results, because in measurable outcomes lies the proof, and in tangible benefit lies goodwill. As scrutiny on this work intensifies, we don't have the luxury of efforts that feel good but do harm; we have to do this work like our organizations and communities are on the line, because let's face it, they are. Coalitions give our work power and legitimacy. If we can rally and organize the huge majority of people who stand to benefit from a more fair, accessible, inclusive, and representative world and communicate a vision of trust, safety, and abundance, we can build a platform and movement that can withstand attack from those peddling fear, threat, and scarcity. And finally, we must communicate well and communicate often about the power of win-win, to push back against the seductive lie that benefiting some requires harming others. By solving real problems and creating real value for real people, we can deliver so much benefit that we take the wind out of extremists' sails.

These tenets give us the path forward and inform the evidence-based practices all of our organizations should be using, not for "committing to FAIR" like we're simply replacing one ideology with another, but truly achieving Fairness, Access, Inclusion, and Representation for all.

Fairness is when an environment has been designed to support all people in succeeding to their full potential, free from discrimination and systemic barriers. We achieve it not by problematizing "biased people" but by collectively solving biases within an environment using the tools of change management.

Access is when all people can fully participate and engage with an experience, environment, product, or service, as a result of their access needs being met. We achieve it not by designing for ourselves and making duct-tape modifications for others, but by bringing our audiences into the design process to create benefits for all.

Inclusion is when all people feel valued, respected, physically safe, and psychologically safe for who they are, across all dimensions of difference. We achieve it by breaking out of identity essentialism, maximalism, glass houses, and small wars, instead building movements that give us all a way to participate and benefit from change.

Representation is when all people trust those who lead them to understand and operate with their needs and interests in mind, regardless of those leaders' social identities. We achieve it not by pursuing tokenistic box-checking but by holding our leaders to high standards of trust built by leading well.

These definitions and these tenets are tools that anyone, anywhere, can carry into their communities and organizations. They are guiding principles that any thoughtful practitioner can use to inform not only the goals they strive toward, but also the tactics they develop and use to solve the vast set of challenges organizations navigating a world defined by difference often encounter.

Pushback and backlash are inevitable in this line of work, and just as they exist, so too does principled resistance. But backlash is evolving quickly, and we have to be willing to evolve in return. The old DEI paradigm is long gone, pulled out from under us almost faster than it appeared following the murder of George Floyd in the summer of 2020. Our charge now is to create in a successor to legacy DEI a framework that achieves the outcomes that DEI could not, addresses the root causes that DEI could not, builds the coalitions DEI failed to build, and communicates the win-win in a way that DEI failed to articulate.

If we can learn from history and the most successful of our last few decades of evidence-based DEI work, we can set ourselves on a trajectory to not only survive this moment but deepen and strengthen the impact we sought to make all along. If we can not only change how we talk about DEI but evolve the substance of the work to become FAIR, we can meaningfully, tangibly change our organizations for the better, for every single one of us. With FAIR, we can do more than commit—we will win.

What are we waiting for?

10 "Black-White Wage Gaps Expand with Rising Wage Inequality," Economic Policy Institute, accessed April 12, 2025, *https://www.epi.org/publication /black-white-wage-gaps-expand-with-rising-wage-inequality/*.

11 Cheryl Winokur Munk, "Workers without Degrees Are Not Getting as Many Good Job Offers as It Seems," CNBC, February 20, 2024, *https:// www.cnbc.com/2024/02/19/job-posts-for-workers-without-degrees-are -booming-but-not-the-hiring.html*.

12 Sarah Aitchison, "Disability and Job Disparities," Atticus, November 16, 2023, *https://www.atticus.com/advice/general/disability-and-job-disparities*.

13 "Monster Poll: Workplace Discrimination," Monster.com, September 6, 2023, *https://hiring.monster.com/resources/blog/monster-poll-workplace -discrimination/*.

14 Jeffrey To, "How Diversity Statements Backfire—and What Orgs Can Do," The Decision Lab, August 5, 2021, *https://thedecisionlab.com/insights/hr /how-diversity-statements-backfire-and-what-organizations-can-do-about-it*.

15 Jordan Whitehouse, "Why Board Gender Quotas Are Nothing to Fear," *Smith Business Insight*, November 14, 2023, *https://smith.queensu.ca/insight /content/Why-Board-Gender-Quotas-Are-Nothing-to-Fear.php*.

16 Andrew Adam Newman, "Target Suffers 10th Consecutive Week of Foot Traffic Declines, Sinking Stock Prices Since Caving on DEI," *Retail Brew*, April 11, 2025, *https://www.retailbrew.com/stories/2025/04/11/target-suffers -10th-consecutive-week-of-foot-traffic-declines-sinking-stock-prices-since-caving -on-dei*.

Chapter 2

1 Christopher Rufo (@realchrisrufo), "We launched the Claudine Gay plagiarism story from the Right. The next step is to smuggle it into the media apparatus of the Left, legitimizing the narrative to center-left actors who have the power to topple her. Then squeeze," X, January 3, 2024, *https:// x.com/realchrisrufo/status/1737209215738069232*.

2 Ian Ward, "We Sat Down with the Conservative Mastermind behind Claudine Gay's Ouster," *Politico*, January 3, 2024, *https://www.politico.com /news/magazine/2024/01/03/christopher-rufo-claudine-gay-harvard -resignation-00133618*.

3 Lily Zheng, "The Failure of the DEI-Industrial-Complex," *Harvard Business Review*, December 1, 2022, *https://hbr.org/2022/12/the-failure-of-the-dei-industrial-complex*.

4 *Human Resource Management—Diversity and Inclusion*, ISO 30415:2021, International Standards Organization, May 2021, *https://www.iso.org/standard/71164.html*.

5 Hoa Briscoe-Tran, "Is DEI Valuable to Investors?," *The CLS Blue Sky Blog*, June 27, 2024, *https://clsbluesky.law.columbia.edu/2024/06/27/is-dei-valuable-to-investors/*.

6 Kelsey Minor, "Three Years after George Floyd's Murder: Where Is DEI Now, and What Have Companies Learned?," *Senior Executive*, March 21, 2023, *https://seniorexecutive.com/three-years-after-george-floyds-murder-where-is-dei-now-and-what-have-companies-learned/*.

7 Elizabeth Levy Paluck et al., "Prejudice Reduction: Progress and Challenges," *Annual Review of Psychology* 72, no. 1 (2021): 533–560.

8 Calvin K. Lai et al., "Reducing Implicit Racial Preferences: I. A Comparative Investigation of 17 Interventions," *Journal of Experimental Psychology: General* 143, no. 4 (2014): 1765.

9 C. Neil Macrae et al., "Out of Mind but Back in Sight: Stereotypes on the Rebound," *Journal of Personality and Social Psychology* 67, no. 5 (1994): 808.

10 Erin Cooley et al., "Complex Intersections of Race and Class: Among Social Liberals, Learning about White Privilege Reduces Sympathy, Increases Blame, and Decreases External Attributions for White People Struggling with Poverty," *Journal of Experimental Psychology: General* 148, no. 12 (2019): 2218.

11 James A. Thomas, "Changes in Black and White Perceptions of the Army's Race Relations/Equal Opportunity Programs—1972 to 1974," ERIC, November 1976, *https://eric.ed.gov/?id=ED144912*.

12 Lisa Legault, Jennifer N. Gutsell, and Michael Inzlicht, "Ironic Effects of Antiprejudice Messages: How Motivational Interventions Can Reduce (but Also Increase) Prejudice," *Psychological Science* 22, no. 12 (2011): 1472–1477.

13 Iris Bohnet, *What Works: Gender Equality by Design* (Harvard University Press, 2016).

14 Frank Dobbin and Alexandra Kalev, "Why Diversity Programs Fail," *Harvard Business Review* 94, no. 7 (2016): 52–60.

15 Frank Dobbin, Daniel Schrage, and Alexandra Kalev, "Rage against the Iron Cage: The Varied Effects of Bureaucratic Personnel Reforms on Diversity," *American Sociological Review* 80, no. 5 (2015): 1014–1044.

16 Lily Zheng, "To Avoid DEI Backlash, Focus on Changing Systems—Not People," *Harvard Business Review*, September 21, 2022.

17 Nella Van Dyke and Bryan Amos, "Social Movement Coalitions: Formation, Longevity, and Success," *Sociology Compass* 11, no. 7 (2017): e12489.

18 Aarti Iyer, "Understanding Advantaged Groups' Opposition to Diversity, Equity, and Inclusion (DEI) Policies: The Role of Perceived Threat," *Social and Personality Psychology Compass* 16, no. 5 (2022): e12666.

Chapter 3

1 Marianne Bertrand and Sendhil Mullainathan, "Are Emily and Greg More Employable Than Lakisha and Jamal? A Field Experiment on Labor Market Discrimination," *American Economic Review* 94, no. 4 (2004): 991–1013.

2 Scott H. Decker et al., "Criminal Stigma, Race, and Ethnicity: The Consequences of Imprisonment for Employment," *Journal of Criminal Justice* 43, no. 2 (2015): 108–121.

3 Patrick Kline, Evan K. Rose, and Christopher R. Walters, "A Discrimination Report Card," The University of Chicago Becker Friedman Institute for Economics, April 8, 2024, *https://bfi.uchicago.edu/insight/research-summary/a-discrimination-report-card/*.

4 "Hiring and Recruiting," Bias Interrupters, January 29, 2023, *https://biasinterrupters.org/hiring/*.

5 Joe Hernandez, "White-Sounding Names Get Called Back for Jobs More Than Black Ones, a New Study Finds," NPR, April 11, 2024, *https://www.npr.org/2024/04/11/1243713272/resume-bias-study-white-names-black-names*.

6 Elizabeth Levy Paluck and Donald P. Green, "Prejudice Reduction: What Works? A Review and Assessment of Research and Practice," *Annual Review of Psychology* 60, no. 1 (2009): 339–367.

7 "Bozoma Saint John: 'I Wanted to Increase the Numbers of Black Women in Tech, So I Did It Myself,'" Women in the World, YouTube, 2019, *https://www.youtube.com/watch?v=Tv6VIKc7_RI*.

8 Madeline E. Heilman and Brian Welle, "Disadvantaged by Diversity? The Effects of Diversity Goals on Competence Perceptions," *Journal of Applied Social Psychology* 36, no. 5 (2006): 1291–1319, *https://doi.org/10.1111 /j.0021-9029.2006.00043.x*.

9 Sandra Portocarrero and James T. Carter, "'But the Fellows Are Simply Diversity Hires!' How Organizational Contexts Influence Status Beliefs," *RSF: The Russell Sage Foundation Journal of the Social Sciences* 8, no. 7 (2022): 172–191.

10 Zoie Diana et al., "Voluntary Commitments Made by the World's Largest Companies Focus on Recycling and Packaging over Other Actions to Address the Plastics Crisis," *One Earth* 5, no. 11 (2022): 1286–1306.

11 Aarti Iyer, "Understanding Advantaged Groups' Opposition to Diversity, Equity, and Inclusion (DEI) Policies: The Role of Perceived Threat," *Social and Personality Psychology Compass* 16, no. 5 (2022): e12666.

12 "To Make Change, Start with a Crowd," SPARQ (Stanford University), accessed April 12, 2025, *https://sparq.stanford.edu/solutions/make-change -start-crowd*.

13 Frank Dobbin and Alexandra Kalev, "Why Diversity Programs Fail," *Harvard Business Review* 94, no. 7 (2016): 14.

Chapter 4

1 Delthia Ricks, "Uprooting Bias in Artificial Intelligence," *Morgan Magazine* (Morgan State University), October 7, 2022, *https://magazine.morgan .edu/artificial-intelligence/*.

2 *Personal Protective Equipment and Women*, Purple Boots Campaign, Women's Engineering Society, January 25, 2018, *https://www.tuc.org.uk/sites /default/files/PPEandwomenguidance.pdf*.

3 Missy Jensen, "Web Accessibility Stats and Data 2024," AudioEye, February 14, 2024, *https://www.audioeye.com/post/accessibility-statistics/*.

4 Cliff Jerrison, "The Missing Stair," *The Pervocracy*, June 22, 2012, *https:// pervocracy.blogspot.com/2012/06/missing-stair.html*.

5 Sasha Costanza-Chock, *Design Justice: Community-Led Practices to Build the Worlds We Need* (MIT Press, 2020), *https://direct.mit.edu/books/oa-monograph /4605/Design-JusticeCommunity-Led-Practices-to-Build-the*.

6 Jiseon Shin and Sang Kyun Kim, "The Egocentrism of Entrepreneurs: Bias in Comparative Judgments," *Entrepreneurship Research Journal* 9, no. 1 (2019): 20170100.

7 Tim Hillegonds, "The Fallacy of Average," Thrive, July 14, 2023, *https://www.thrivecs.com/insights/the-fallacy-of-average*.

8 Yuhan Xu, "Dolce & Gabbana Ad (with Chopsticks) Provokes Public Outrage in China," NPR, December 1, 2018, *https://www.npr.org/sections/goatsandsoda/2018/12/01/671891818/dolce-gabbana-ad-with-chopsticks-provokes-public-outrage-in-china*.

9 Karen Korellis Reuther, "Shrink It and Pink It: Gender Bias in Product Design," *Harvard Advanced Leadership Initiative Social Impact Review*, October 25, 2022, *https://www.sir.advancedleadership.harvard.edu/articles/shrink-it-and-pink-it-gender-bias-product-design*.

10 Caroline Casey, "Do Your D&I Efforts Include People with Disabilities?," *Harvard Business Review*, March 19, 2020, *https://hbr.org/2020/03/do-your-di-efforts-include-people-with-disabilities*.

11 *Global Economics of Disability Report: 2024*, The Return on Disability Group, September 24, 2024, *https://www.rod-group.com/wp-content/uploads/2024/09/The-Global-Economics-of-Disability-2024-The-Return-on-Disability-Group-September-24-2024.pdf*.

12 Angela Glover Blackwell, "The Curb-Cut Effect (SSIR)," *Stanford Social Innovation Review*, 2017, *https://ssir.org/articles/entry/the_curb_cut_effect*.

13 Julie Peterson, "Smashing Barriers to Access: Disability Activism and Curb Cuts," National Museum of American History, July 15, 2015, *https://americanhistory.si.edu/explore/stories/smashing-barriers-access-disability-activism-and-curb-cuts*.

14 Alicia Koontz et al., "'Nothing about Us without Us:' Engaging AT Users in AT Research," *Assistive Technology* 34, no. 5 (2022): 499–500, *https://doi.org/10.1080/10400435.2022.2117524*.

Chapter 5

1 Maurice Mitchell, "Building Resilient Organizations," Forge: Organizing Strategy and Practice, November 29, 2022, *https://forgeorganizing.org/article/building-resilient-organizations/*.

2 adrienne maree brown, "A Call to Attention Liberation: To Build Abundant Justice, Let's Focus on What Matters," *Truthout*, March 16, 2018, *https://truthout.org/articles/a-call-to-attention-liberation-to-build-abundant-justice-let-s-focus-on-what-matters/*.

3 Sarah McKenna et al., "Are Diverse Societies Less Cohesive? Testing Contact and Mediated Contact Theories," *PLOS ONE* 13, no. 3 (2018): e0193337, *https://doi.org/10.1371/journal.pone.0193337*.

4 Lisa H. Nishii, "The Benefits of Climate for Inclusion for Gender-Diverse Groups," *Academy of Management Journal* 56, no. 6 (2013): 1754–1774, *https://doi.org/10.5465/amj.2009.0823*.

5 Audre Lorde, *Sister Outsider: Essays and Speeches* (Crossing Press, 2012), *https://wlrc.uic.edu/news-stories/we-do-not-live-single-issue-lives/*.

6 Janet Ward Schofield, "Causes and Consequences of the Colorblind Perspective," in *Prejudice, Discrimination, and Racism*, ed. John F. Dovidio (Academic Press, 1986), 231–253.

7 Akshaj Kumar Veldanda et al., "Are Emily and Greg Still More Employable Than Lakisha and Jamal? Investigating Algorithmic Hiring Bias in the Era of ChatGPT," arXiv preprint arXiv:2310.05135 (2023).

8 Christopher Wolsko et al., "Framing Interethnic Ideology: Effects of Multicultural and Color-Blind Perspectives on Judgments of Groups and Individuals," *Journal of Personality and Social Psychology* 78, no. 4 (2000): 635.

9 john a. powell, "Targeted Universalism," Othering & Belonging Institute, February 21, 2020, *https://belonging.berkeley.edu/targeted-universalism*.

10 Karin Sanders et al., "Employees' Organizational Solidarity within Modern Organizations: A Framing Perspective on the Effects of Social Embeddedness," *Solidarity and Prosocial Behavior: An Integration of Sociological and Psychological Perspectives* (2006): 141–156, *https://doi.org/10.1007/0-387-28032-4_9*.

11 Lynn Farrell et al., "When You Put It That Way: Framing Gender Equality Initiatives to Improve Engagement among STEM Academics," *BioScience* 71, no. 3 (2021): 292–304, *https://doi.org/10.1093/biosci/biaa136*.

12 Elizabeth Levy Paluck, Hana Shepherd, and Peter M. Aronow, "Changing Climates of Conflict: A Social Network Experiment in 56 Schools," *Proceedings of the National Academy of Sciences* 113, no. 3 (2016): 566–571, *https://doi.org/10.1073/pnas.1514483113*.

Chapter 6

1 Pamela Newkirk, "Diversity Has Become a Booming Business. So Where Are the Results?," *Time*, October 10, 2019, *https://time.com/5696943/diversity-business/*.

2 Ted Kennedy Jr., "Increasing Disability Representation on Corporate Boards," *Directors & Boards*, July 13, 2023, *https://www.directorsandboards.com/board-composition/board-diversity/increasing-disability-representation-on-corporate-boards*.

3 Katherine Schaeffer, "119th Congress Brings New Growth in Racial, Ethnic Diversity to Capitol Hill," Pew Research Center, January 21, 2025, *https://www.pewresearch.org/short-reads/2025/01/21/119th-congress-brings-new-growth-in-racial-ethnic-diversity-to-capitol-hill/*.

4 Emma Hinchliffe, "The Share of Fortune 500 Companies Run by Women CEOs Stays Flat at 10.4% as Pace of Change Stalls," *Fortune*, June 4, 2024, *https://fortune.com/2024/06/04/fortune-500-companies-women-ceos-2024/*.

5 Sara Ashley O'Brien, "He's Served on 14 Boards. Now He Wants Companies to Find Other Black Candidates," *CNN Business*, July 24, 2020, *https://perma.cc/XKD4-YRLF*.

6 Ethan Moon, Yangyang Li, and Claire McMahon, "One and Done? Evidence of Gender and Racial Tokenism on Corporate Boards," SSRN (2023), *http://dx.doi.org/10.2139/ssrn.4694128*.

7 Martin Luther King Jr., "The Case against 'Tokenism,'" *New York Times Magazine*, August 5, 1962, *https://archivesspace.bu.edu/repositories/9/archival_objects/101742*.

8 Michael Bailey, "Tokenism," in *Diversity, Equity, and Inclusion in Veterinary Medicine* (Wiley, 2025), 215–228, *https://doi.org/10.1002/9781394217113.ch20*.

9 Denise Lewin Loyd and Lisa M. Amoroso, "Undermining Diversity: Favoritism Threat and Its Effect on Advocacy for Similar Others," *Group Dynamics: Theory, Research, and Practice* 22, no. 3 (2018): 143, *https://doi.org/10.1037/gdn0000087*.

10 Kelly Danaher and Nyla R. Branscombe, "Maintaining the System with Tokenism: Bolstering Individual Mobility Beliefs and Identification with a Discriminatory Organization," *British Journal of Social Psychology* 49, no. 2 (2010): 343–362, *https://doi.org/10.1348/014466609X457530*.

11 Chuck Shelton, "The Study on White Men Leading through Diversity & Inclusion," Greatheart Consulting, December 7, 2013, *https://static1 .squarespace.com/static/5fa09c714da1e52de477c6bf/t/5fdd0946955ca97240f 961ff/1608321355340/Executive+Summary.pdf.*

12 Sam Kaner, *Facilitator's Guide to Participatory Decision-Making* (John Wiley & Sons, 2014).

13 Giselle A. Auger, "Trust Me, Trust Me Not: An Experimental Analysis of the Effect of Transparency on Organizations," *Journal of Public Relations Research* 26, no. 4 (2014): 325–343, *https://doi.org/10.1080/1062726X .2014.908722.*

Chapter 7

1 Heather Graci, "Most Americans Dislike Income Inequality. But They Disagree about Who Should Fix It," *Behavioral Scientist*, March 2, 2025, *https://behavioralscientist.org/most-americans-dislike-income-inequality-but -they-disagree-about-who-should-fix-it/.*

2 Gabriel Borelli, "Americans Are Split over the State of the American Dream," Pew Research Center, July 2, 2024, *https://www.pewresearch.org /short-reads/2024/07/02/americans-are-split-over-the-state-of-the-american -dream/.*

3 Justin Gomer and Christopher Petrella, "How the Reagan Administration Stoked Fears of Anti-White Racism," *The Washington Post*, October 10, 2017, *https://www.washingtonpost.com/news/made-by-history/wp/2017/10 /10/how-the-reagan-administration-stoked-fears-of-anti-white-racism/.*

4 Jeremy Herb et al., "Trump Is Using the Power of Government to Punish Opponents. They're Struggling to Respond," *CNN Politics*, March 30, 2025, *https://www.cnn.com/2025/03/30/politics/trump-punish-opponents /index.html.*

ACKNOWLEDGMENTS

To my best friend and wife, Andrea: thank you from the bottom of my heart. I could not have written this book without your love and support. From cracking my back after a midnight writing session to your companionship during the tough moments to leaving little Post-its around the house to keep me motivated, your kindness and thoughtfulness leave me speechless. I love you, and I'm so grateful for everything you do for us. I'm also keeping all the Post-its.

To Rich, Reena, Cynder, Danger, Kristen, Emmy, Neon, and many others, thank you for your time, your companionship, your joy, and your care throughout the grueling process of writing a book. I wouldn't be able to do what I do without my community.

To Tracy, my longtime friend, colleague, and calendar-wrangler extraordinaire: whew. Thank you. I promise I'll get to all the other tasks on the calendar that I've asked you to put aside now that this is done.

To Brian, who helped me with some of the extensive literature review and research that supports this book, thank you. If I could have had my way we would have included several hundred more of your references. Even if they didn't make it into the book, I'll be sure to try and read through all the articles you compiled—can't take me longer than a year to get through them. Probably.

To Jeevan, my insightful and ever-so-patient editor: thanks for holding me accountable and for being understanding when I missed our first book deadline. You'd think by the fifth rodeo I'd have gotten better at this, huh?

To the no less than five local coffee shops that have kept me caffeinated through my writing trials, thank you. To Jovanna, Hauz, and Walter at the place down the street, thank you specifically for brightening up my day, day after day, both pre- and post-caffeination. Couldn't have done it without you!

And to you, dear reader, thank you for coming with me on this journey. If you've made it this far, know that as much as it's my job to find the words, I truly don't have the means to express my gratitude to you here. Thank you for engaging with these vulnerable ideas. May they help you navigate the challenges ahead.

INDEX

A

absolutism, 97–98
abundance mindset, 10, 46, 106
access for all
    and accessibility, 75, 83
    curb cut effect, 82–83, 89
    vs. duct tape "solutions", 77, 80–81
    in FAIR Framework, 7
    inclusive/universal design, 83–84
    legacy DEI equivalents, 12
    meeting needs for, 73–74
    as a smart investment, 12
    systemic change for, 87–90
    user input to design, 84–87
accountability
    via data, 68
    lack of legacy DEI, 11, 38
    normalizing, 70
    organizational disinterest in, 42
affirmative action programs, 25, 129
ageism, 28, 75
allies, 98–99, 104–105
Amazon, 23
American Dream, 127–128
antidiscrimination laws, 24, 28

antiracism protests, 41
Asian people, 28, 112, 120
assessments, employee, 20, 46, 50, 64,
    103, 123
"average," as nonexistent, 12

B

backlash, anti-DEI
    antagonistic language of, 9, 10, 37
    against cultural events, 93
    current climate of, 130
    drivers of, 65, 97
    and focus on individuals, 57,
      60–62
    as inevitable, 134
    as the minority group, 38
    from moving too fast, 65
    one-off DEI training as seed of,
      43, 45
    personal hurts as root of, 38
    playbook for, 35–36
    Romeo and Juliet effect, 67–68
    solution to, 3, 39, 51, 94
    targets of, 35, 37
    transformation of, 34

beliefs
    awareness of your, 86
    prioritizing your, 85
    rallying change in, 66
belonging, 132
Bertrand, Marianne, 53
best practices lists, 18, 64, 86
bias
    awareness of your, 86
    egocentric bias, 79
    exacerbation of, 44
    individual vs. systemic, 54–55
binaries, moving beyond, 101
Black people
    affirmative action for, 129
    anti-Black racism protests, 41
    hiring discrimination, 28, 53–54,
        58–59
    ineffectiveness of DEI for, 4–5
    representation for, 112
    wage gaps for, 28
boardmember gender quotas, 31
brown, adrienne marie, 100
"Building Resilient Organizations"
    (Mitchell), 95
burnout, workplace, 7, 30
bystander intervention, 60

C

celebrating success, 70–71
changemaking
    abundance mindset for, 46
    aversion to large-scale, 21
    barriers to effective, 94–101,
        128–129
    call for, 127
    vs. comfort/safety, 8

designing solutions, 66
    of the environment, 9, 60–62,
        64–71
    four methods for effective, 31–33
    glass houses/small wars in, 99
    idealism about, 28
    identifying as changemakers, 13
    identity and movement building,
        101–102
    maximalism in, 97–98
    rallying, 65, 88–89
    via representation, 120
    resistance to, 67–68, 87, 88
    role of conflict in, 100
    stakeholder/user input into,
        84–87
    systemic vs. individual, 60–62
    tokenism vs., 117
    vs. tolerating inappropriateness,
        78, 87–88
    tools to accelerate, 70
    via tracking DEI impact, 45
    unintended consequences of,
        16–17, 18
    to workplace culture, 48–49
change management, 66
Civil Rights Act of 1964, 24, 28, 59
coalitions
    cliques vs., 132
    collective action by, 107, 133
    competition vs., 47–48, 100
    inclusion via, 94
    maximalism vs., 98–99
    positive impact via creating, 46
    to transform DEI backlash, 34
cobra effect, 15–17, 111
"colorblindness", 101

comfort, 8
communication
    identity essentialism in, 95–97
    respectful, 17
    substantive debate, 97
community
    designing for the, 79
    ERGs to build workplace, 91–93
    group identity vs., 101
    outside of work, 32, 33
competition, 31, 47–48
conflict, productive, 100
consumer action, 32
Costanza-Chock, Sasha, 78
cultural changes, 48–49
cultural heritage celebrations, 5,
    91–93
curb cut effect, 82, 84, 86, 89

D
data analytics, 45
data as accountability, 68
DEI Deconstructed, 27
DEI initiatives
    assessing outcomes of, 103
    call for silver bullets in, 17–18
    celebrating successful, 70–71
    DEI acronym vilification, 3
    done right, 10, 39, 130
    effective, 3–4, 31–33
    enshittification of, 24, 29
    fear of anti-DEI backlash in, 37
    history/origins of, 24–25, 129
    individual vs. systemic, 56–57
    iterative, 69
    lip service initiatives, 26–27
    majority support for, 2, 38

mistakes made in, 18–19
    negative experiences with, 38
    one-off DEI trainings, 43
    post–George Floyd DEI boom,
        41–42
    practical progress via, 6–7
    scaling up, 69
    storytelling to rally change,
        65–66
    trust in, 113
    U.S. government dismantling
        of, 1
    U.S. statistics on support for, 2,
        130
    value of industry, 29
    See also legacy DEI; workplace
        DEI
democracy, pluralistic, 1
demographic analyses, 64
demographic representation, 13
desegregation, 25
designing solutions
    access as good design, 73
    for change, 66
    for the collective, 78–79, 118
    curb cut effect, 82–83
    differences accounted for
        in, 84
    for fairness for all, 57
    needs-first approach to, 75
    partners/stakeholders in, 77
    stakeholder/user input into,
        84–87
    See also problem solving
*Design Justice: Community-Led
    Practices to Build the Worlds We
    Need* (Costanza-Chock), 78

differences in identity
    accessibility for various, 84
    and collective benefit, 9
    embracing all, 124
    erasure of, 101
    fear of sharing amidst, 38
    finding solidarity amidst, 97, 100
    organizing across, 93
    positive conflict and, 100
disability
    accessibility and, 75, 82–83
    board members with, 112
    curb cut effect, 82–83
    designing for, 80
    discrimination based on, 28–29, 59
disconnect, right to, 50
discrimination
    affirmative action and reduced, 25
    antidiscrimination laws, 24
    bystander intervention in, 60
    "colorblindness", 101
    disability-related, 81
    in hiring, 28, 53, 56, 58–59
    and identity essentialism, 97
    by industry, 56
    via one-off DEI trainings, 44–45
    paying lip service to, 26–27
    vs. performative cultural events,
      92
    "positive", 58, 60
    "reverse", 6
    social toleration of, 2
    systemic, 54–55
    wage gaps, 28
diversity
    "diversity hires", 59
    history of activism for, 129

ineffective diversity training, 27
    lip service to, 30
    pro-diversity U.S. statistics, 2
    pro-diversity vs. pro-DEI, 3
    in the workplace, 5
divisiveness, 1, 2, 11
Doctorow, Cory, 22, 31
duct tape "solutions", 77, 80–81

E

egocentric bias, 79, 85, 107
employee resource groups (ERGs),
    30, 32, 40, 46, 91
engagement survey, 5, 46
enshittification, 22–24, 29, 30, 31, 32,
    34, 43
environment
    changing the, 9, 57, 62
    culture of inclusion, 94
    fairness in, 12, 53, 55
    scaling change across, 69–70
    systemic change in, 78, 87–90
    systemic discrimination, 54–55
    tracking results to change, 45
    understanding of, 67
equal employment opportunity
    (EEO) training, 24–25
Equal Employment Opportunity
    Commission (EEOC), 24
equity
    via affirmative action programs,
      25
    via boardmember gender quotas,
      31
    call for, 127–128
    declines in, 27
    DEI as distinct from, 3, 5

history of activism for, 129
presumed in legacy DEI work, 27
representational parity, 114
in the workplace, 5
everyone
access for all, 75–76, 89
changemaking for, 102–108
fairness for, 7–8, 51, 63
representational parity for, 114
respect for, 94
targeted universalism,
102–104, 105
exclusion, social toleration of, 2
executives
Black male, 112
in culture of overwork, 48, 49
female, 31, 51
representational parity
among, 124

F

Facebook, 21, 22, 23
FAIR (Fairness, Access, Inclusion,
and Representation) Framework
access in, 74–75, 77, 82
barriers to, 94–95
as DEI done right, 10, 33
as environmental, 55
for everyone, 7–8, 51
fixing DEI flaws via, 9
inclusion in, 94
legacy DEI equivalents, 12
overcoming resistance to, 87
practical progress via, 128
reinventing legacy DEI via,
12–13, 132
representation in, 111

tenets of, 46, 133–134
trust in, 113, 122
fairness
as American ideal, 127
building fair organizations,
62–63
environmental, 53
in FAIR Framework, 7
fighting fire with fire for, 58
incentivizing, 55
legacy DEI equivalents, 12
representational parity, 114,
124–125
vs. "self-advocacy", 29–30
systemic design for, 57
fear of anti-DEI backlash, 37
feedback, 69, 77, 121
financial repercussions
competition, 31
of pro-DEI reputation, 41
of regulatory (non)compliance, 31
Fixing Fairness, 7
Floyd, George, 41, 42

G

Gallup, 28
Gay, Claudine, 35
gender issues
access for all, 75
boardmember gender quotas, 31
DEI initiatives worsening, 46–47
disparity reduction, 51
gendered product ads, 79
inclusion-effort mistakes, 18
role assignments, 64–65
glass houses/small wars, 95,
99–100

good intentions
    bad effects from, 15–17, 19,
        34, 131
    glass houses/small wars and,
        99–100
    paired with harmful tactics, 58,
        60, 62
    tracking results vs., 45
    without accountability, 11
Google, 24
"green" language, 26

H
harm
    of legacy DEI, 6, 44
    no free pass to do, 118–119
    of sixty-minute DEI training, 43
    tokenism and replication of, 117
Harvard University, 35
Hillegonds, Tom, 79
hiring
    circumventing the process of,
        58–59
    DEI lip service in, 30
    discrimination, 28, 53, 56, 58–59
    fair, 114
    inspecting practices of, 121
    standardizing, 56
    turnover rate and, 87
hope, 1, 2, 127
hybrid work, 48, 80

I
identities/social groups
    and backlash drivers, 65
    celebration of all, 13
    designing for various, 77–78

desire for value among, 105–106
    differences in, 9
    identity and movement building,
        101–102
    overlapping silos of, 104
    performative celebrations of,
        91–93
    "privileged", 44
    raising expectations of, 118
    rallying change among, 66
    representational parity for
        all, 114
    silver bullets for relating to, 17–18
    targeted universalism for,
        102–104
    token representation of, 115–117
    trust by/of, 111
    value neutrality on, 104
    worsening tension between
        groups, 44
identity essentialism, 95–97, 110,
    117, 120
ideology, 5, 6, 38, 100
impact of DEI
    activities vs., 20–21, 27
    ignoring, 131
    leadership disinterest in, 42
    measuring, 45, 68–69, 133
    targeted universalism and,
        102–104
    trust surveys, 122–123
inclusion
    assessing outcomes of, 103
    DEI as distinct from, 3, 5
    environmental, 94, 100
    for everyone, 102–104, 105, 106
    failed initiatives, 91–93

in FAIR Framework, 7, 94
goal of, 93
history of activism for, 129
in legacy DEI work, 12, 27
reinventing, 13
as a smart investment, 12
as solidarity at scale, 91
in the workplace, 5
inclusive design, 83–84
income gaps, 28–29
inequality
    demographic analyses of, 64
    eliminating environmental,
        62–63
    hiring discrimination, 54–56
    identifying present of, 64–65
    persistence of workplace, 21
    in promotion times, 64–65
    systemic address to, 56–58
    tokenism to maintain, 116
Instagram, 22
inter-identity coalitions, 12
intra-identity cliques, 12
iterative initiatives, 69

J

Jerrison, Cliff, 78
justice, designing for, 78

K

King, Martin Luther, Jr., 115
Kline, Pat, 56

L

labor, influence of, 31, 32
language access, 75
Latino people, 28, 112

leadership
    DEI idealism among, 28
    DEI jitters among, 3
    effective/efficient, 49
    engaged in change, 67–68
    ERG, 92
    marginalized groups in, 112
    vs. overworked workers, 48
    polarization defused by, 11
    representational parity in, 124
    of the status quo, 117
    trust in, 13, 122
    turnover and dysfunctional, 87
    by women/for women, 109–110
leave policies, 76
Lee, N'Tanya, 100
legacy DEI
    accessibility in, 75, 77
    activities vs. impact in, 20–21,
        27, 42
    disability failures in, 81
    enshittification of, 29, 43–44
    FAIR Framework vs., 52
    and flatlined antidiscrimination,
        28
    flaws in, 8, 9, 131–132
    harm done by, 6
    identity essentialism in, 97
    individual focus in, 57, 60–62
    ineffectiveness of, 4–6, 11, 27, 39
    maximalism in, 99
    overlapping silos in, 101–102,
        104
    performative, 6, 8, 10, 20–21, 40,
        43, 112, 131
    as regulatory compliance, 24
    reinventing, 7, 12, 120, 132, 134

legacy DEI
    representation and, 111,
        113, 123
    vilification of, 1
    zero-sum mindset of, 10
Lewin, Kurt, 66, 67
life outside of work, 48, 50
lip service initiatives, 6, 8, 21, 40

M

marginalized groups
    and access for all, 75–76
    affirmative action programs
        for, 25
    backlash against, 37, 45
    curb cut effect, 82–83, 89
    desire for value among, 105–106
    ERGs for, 91–92
    Oppression Olympics among, 40,
        95–97, 100
    performative DEI vs., 41
    representation of, 112, 114
    stereotypes of, 44, 79, 102
    targeted universalism and,
        102–104
    tokenism of, 115–117
    trust by/of, 111
    undervaluing of, 114
    wage gaps for, 28–29
    See also group identity by name
maximalism, 95, 97–99
McCall, Leslie, 127
Mead, Margaret, 66
measuring impact, 45, 68–69,
    123, 133
media platforms, 22–24
men

backlash by, 93
    polarization against women,
        46–48
    privileged accommodation
        for, 48
meritocracy, 37, 63
Meta, 22
Middle Eastern/North African
    people, 28, 112
mindsets
    of abundance vs. zero-sum, 10,
        46, 106, 113
    changemaker, 13
"missing stair", 78, 87
Mitchell, Maurice, 95, 99, 106
Mullainathan, Sendhil, 53

N

nepotism, 58

O

one-off DEI trainings, 43, 57, 106
Oppression Olympics, 95–101
organizational solidarity, 107–108
organizations
    access for all at, 75–77
    affirmative action programs at,
        24–26
    anti-bias policies in, 56
    antidiscrimination reputation of,
        26–27, 40
    changing culture at, 48–49
    corporate cover-ups, 61
    decision-making method in, 80
    dysfunctional management of, 87
    enshittification of, 22–24, 29
    executive leadership of, 112

lack of trust at, 32
performative DEI at, 20
policies for fair, 62–63
practicing collective benefit, 11
racism-ending commitments
    by, 41
scaling change in, 69
smart social investments for, 12
as social microcosms, 128
tokenism at, 115
outrage, via social media, 22
overwork, 17, 48

P

pay-equity audits, 20, 99
perfection, interpersonal, 99
performative DEI initiatives, 6, 8, 10,
    20–21, 42–43
Pew Research Center, 3, 127
pluralistic democracy, 1
polarization, 1, 2, 11
political positions, 95
Politico, 35
pollution, 61
Pope, Alexander, 19
positive discrimination, 60
powell, john a., 102
practical progress
    via affirmative action programs,
        25
    via DEI initiatives, 6–7
    in FAIR Framework, 9, 128
    four methods for, 31–33
    vs. impressions of progress, 40
    vs. short-term gains, 22, 29
praise/recognition, 70
principled struggle, 100

"privileged" identities, 44, 45
problem solving
    and the cobra effect, 15–16, 19
    duct tape "solutions", 73–74, 77
    egocentric bias in, 79
    environmental understanding
        for, 67
    rewarding efficient, 50
    rushing into, 65
    stakeholder/user input into,
        84–87
    via systemic change, 78, 87–90
    trust for, 121–122
    See also designing solutions
promotions, 64–65
ProPublica, 28

R

racial phrenology, 40
racial quotas, 6
racism
    hiring discrimination, 53–54
    protests demanding end to, 41
    "reverse", 129
rallying change via stories, 65
Reagan administration, 129
Regents of the University of California v.
    Bakke, 129
regulation, DEI, 24, 31, 33
remote work, 48, 80
representation
    defined, 109
    in FAIR Framework, 7
    impossibility of perfect, 120
    legacy DEI equivalents, 12
    tokenism vs. true, 112, 115–117
    and trust, 111, 113, 120

representational parity, 114, 124
respect
    in communication, 17
    for everyone, 94
    universal desire for, 105
right-wing extremists, 1, 35, 51, 112,
    130
risk aversion, 89
Romeo and Juliet effect, 67
Rufo, Christopher, 35, 37

S

safety, 8, 94, 107
Saint John, Bozoma, 58, 59
self-help, 8, 11, 31, 33, 132
short-term gains, 22, 29, 34
silver bullets, 18
sixty-minute DEI training, 43
slowing down, 17
small utopianism, 100
social media
    platform enshittification on, 22
    rage baiting on, 22
    vilification of DEI on, 1
society
    anti-Black racism protests in, 41
    cobra effect in, 16
    collective shift of, 34
    curb cut effect benefits to,
        82–83, 89
    norms to support status quo in, 8
    organizations as microcosms
        of, 128
solidarity, organizational, 107
standardization of hiring, 56
status quo
    backlash to changing, 37
    call for changing, 127

cost of, 87
fundamental change to, 18
harm done by, 34
leaders of, 117
of overwork, 48–49
powers supporting, 8
tokenism to maintain, 116–117
of workplace DEI, 38
stereotypes
    designs based on, 79
    strengthening of, 44, 102
storytelling to rally change, 65
success, celebrating, 70–71

T

Target, 32
targeted universalism, 102–103
tokenism, 13, 112, 115–117
tolerance, 100
transgender people, 93
trauma porn, 81
trust
    as constant journey, 122
    vs. enshittification, 32
    importance of, 99
    vs. lack of change, 81
    of leaders, 13, 118
    one-off DEI trainings vs., 44
    in organizational solidarity, 107
    in representation, 111, 113, 120
    slowing down to build, 17
    surveys on, 123

U

UC Berkeley Othering and
    Belonging Institute, 102
unintended consequences, 16–17, 111
United States government, 1

universal design, 83–84
University of California, Berkeley, 56
University of Chicago, 56
University of Wisconsin–Madison, 2
unrigging the game, 62–71
Urban Institute, 28
user experience, enshittification and, 23
utopianism, small, 100

V

valued, desire to be, 105, 114
value neutrality, 104

W

wage gaps, 28–29
WhatsApp, 22
White people
    backlash by, 93
    discrimination against, 6
    leadership by, 112
    preferential hiring of, 28, 53–54
    raising expectations of, 118
women
    affirmative action programs for, 25
    boardmember gender quotas, 31
    executives, 109, 112
    hiring discrimination, 58–59
    representation for, 109–110
    wage gape for, 28
    work assigned to, 64
workers
    call for anti-racism initiatives, 41
    "diversity hires", 59
    fairness for all, 63
    life outside work, 48, 50
    performative DEI vs., 41

Working Families Party, 95
work-life balance, 48–49
workplace DEI
    accessibility in, 75
    assessing outcomes of, 103
    contentious initiatives for, 3
    effective, 11
    ERGs to carry out, 91–93
    fear of anti-DEI backlash in, 37
    flaws in, 8–9
    history of self-regulated, 26–27
    identity essentialism in, 97
    individual vs. systemic, 56–57
    ineffective, 11, 20–21, 34, 43–44
    jitters among leadership over, 3
    lip service initiatives, 6
    negative experiences with, 38
    reframing/redefining, 5, 39
    self-regulation and explosion of, 27
    standardizing, 41
    systemic vs. individual focus, 60–62
    value of industry, 29
    vilification of, 1
    See also legacy DEI
workplaces
    access for all in, 75–76
    Amazon, 23
    burnout in, 7
    "colorblind", 101
    inclusive, diverse, 7

Y

YouGov, 3, 4

Z

zero-sum mindset, 10, 13, 46, 113

ABOUT THE AUTHOR

LILY ZHENG (they/them) is a no-nonsense strategist, consultant, and author who helps leaders and practitioners build fair, accessible, inclusive, and representative organizations for everyone. Lily's work has been featured in *Harvard Business Review*, *The New York Times*, and NPR. They are the author of *DEI Deconstructed*, *Reconstructing DEI*, and enough posts on LinkedIn to constitute at least another book. They live in the San Francisco Bay Area, California.

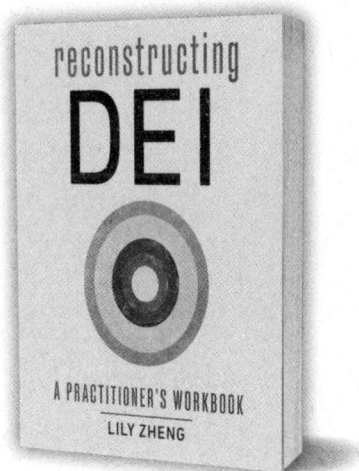

Berrett-Koehler
PUBLISHERS

Berrett-Koehler is an independent publisher dedicated to an ambitious mission: *Connecting people and ideas to create a world that works for all.*

Our publications span many formats, including print, digital, audio, and video. We also offer online resources, training, and gatherings. And we will continue expanding our products and services to advance our mission.

We believe that the solutions to the world's problems will come from all of us, working at all levels: in our society, in our organizations, and in our own lives. Our publications and resources offer pathways to creating a more just, equitable, and sustainable society. They help people make their organizations more humane, democratic, diverse, and effective (and we don't think there's any contradiction there). And they guide people in creating positive change in their own lives and aligning their personal practices with their aspirations for a better world.

And we strive to practice what we preach through what we call "The BK Way." At the core of this approach is *stewardship*, a deep sense of responsibility to administer the company for the benefit of all of our stakeholder groups, including authors, customers, employees, investors, service providers, sales partners, and the communities and environment around us. Everything we do is built around stewardship and our other core values of *quality*, *partnership*, *inclusion*, and *sustainability*.

We are grateful to our readers, authors, and other friends who are supporting our mission. We ask you to share with us examples of how BK publications and resources are making a difference in your lives, organizations, and communities at bkconnection.com/impact.

Dear reader,

Thank you for picking up this book and welcome to the worldwide BK community! You're joining a special group of people who have come together to create positive change in their lives, organizations, and communities.

What's BK all about?

Our mission is to connect people and ideas to create a world that works for all.

Why? Our communities, organizations, and lives get bogged down by old paradigms of self-interest, exclusion, hierarchy, and privilege. But we believe that can change. That's why we seek the leading experts on these challenges—and share their actionable ideas with you.

A welcome gift

To help you get started, we'd like to offer you a free copy of one of our bestselling ebooks:

bkconnection.com/welcome

When you claim your **free ebook**, you'll also be subscribed to our blog.

Our freshest insights

Access the best new tools and ideas for leaders at all levels on our blog at ideas.bkconnection.com.

Sincerely,
Your friends at Berrett-Koehler